Life in YORK *one hundred years ago*

Paul Chrystal and Ian Drake

Photographs from the Hanstock Collection

To the memory of Hugh Murray (1923–2013)

First published in 2021
by Palatine Books,
Carnegie House,
Chatsworth Road
Lancaster LA1 4SL
www.palatinebooks.com

British Library Cataloguing-in-Publication data
A catalogue record for this book is available from the British Library

Paperback ISBN 13: 978-1-910837-32-0

Designed and typeset by Carnegie Book Production
www.carnegiebookproduction.com

Printed and bound by Halstan

Other publications by the Yorkshire Architectural & York Archaeological Society (YAYAS) can be found at 'yayas.org.uk'. See www.paulchrystal.com for further works by Paul Chrystal

Contents

ഐ About the authors ഐ

Paul Chrystal has Classics degrees from the Universities of Hull and Southampton. After almost 40 years of working in medical publishing, he now combines this with writing features for national newspapers and history magazines, as well as appearing regularly on BBC local radio, on the BBC World Service and Radio Four's PM programme. In 2018 Paul contributed to a six-part series for BBC Two 'celebrating the history of some of Britain's most iconic craft industries', in this case chocolate in York. He has been history advisor for a number of York tourist attractions and is the author of approximately 100 books on a wide range of subjects, including many on York and Yorkshire. He is a regular reviewer for and contributor to *Classics for All*, and a contributor to the Classics section of OUP's *Oxford Bibliographies Online*. He is History Editor of the *Yorkshire Archaeological Journal*, the journal of the Yorkshire Archaeological Society and is guest speaker for the prestigious Vassar College New York's London Programme in association with Goldsmith University. Paul lives in Haxby, York. In 2021 Paul was part of the research team for an episode of *Who Do You Think You Are?* set in York and due to air in 2022. www.paulchrystal.com.

Ian Drake is an old boy of Archbishop Holgate's Grammar School and has lived in the York area for over half a century. He is the Keeper of the Evelyn Collection for the Yorkshire Architectural and York Archaeological Society and is an active member of the Association of Voluntary Guides for the City of York and York Archaeological Trust. He is the Honorary Treasurer and Trustee for the Council of British Archaeology Yorkshire. He regularly gives talks to many organisations in the area on a series of York related topics.

ᴓ Acknowledgements ᴓ

Hᴀɴsᴛᴏᴄᴋ ꜰᴀᴍɪʟʏ ᴀᴘᴀʀᴛ, ᴛʜɪs ʙᴏᴏᴋ ʜᴀs been immeasurably improved by the support of a number of people and organisations. The support of the Council and members of Yorkshire Architectural and York Archaeological Society is much appreciated by the authors, not least Sandra Garside-Neville, the Society's Archivist, who methodically and painstakingly digitised many of the images you see in this book. Particular thanks to the Society's Chairman John Shaw and member David Poole who provided invaluable information by identifying some of the events, places and people featured in the collections of photographs. Also to Graham Wilford, Chief Engineer and latterly Managing Director of York Waterworks, for sharing his encyclopaedic knowledge of the company. Thanks to Laura Yeoman and the staff of York Explore for their assistance and permission to include the images from the city archives on page 9 and Steve Lewis of The York Press for permission to reproduce the image on page 11. The wedding photograph on page 10 is reproduced by kind permission of Peter Stanhope.

⋰⋱ Foreword ⋰⋱

IF YOU HAVE EVER WISHED TO see a beautiful city like York through the eyes of our ancestors, old photographs are the obvious way. For over 175 years the Yorkshire Architectural and York Archaeological Society (YAYAS) has developed from a well-meaning group of Anglican clergymen dedicated to the preservation of the city's remaining medieval churches, to a group of architects, historians, archaeologists and enthusiasts. There have been many significant members through the years, such as Florence Wright (1910–86) for many years the Secretary of YAYAS; Hugh Murray (1923–2013) and Doctor William Arthur Evelyn (1860–1935).

The first time I encountered the photographs of Thomas Hanstock would have been at the Castle Museum in York in 1970. As a pupil of Scarcroft Primary School I was taken with my classmates to lectures by Florence Wright who was using a huge Aldis slide projector. I would sit in wonder at those old images; lost buildings and street scenes from the previous hundred years. Little did I realise that almost fifty years later I would be writing a foreword as Chairman of the Yorkshire Architectural and York Archaeological Society. As I sat there in 1970 I was not aware that Florence Wright was the Secretary of YAYAS, and that she had joined the society when Doctor William Arthur Evelyn was still alive. That's how close we are to history; just a meeting or an image away.

Dr William Arthur Evelyn (1860–1935) came to work as a doctor in York in 1891 and fell in love with the city. We have much to thank him for: preventing what remains of the moats outside the incomparable city walls from being filled in, writing memoranda to the City Corporation to stop a view from being destroyed, or preventing advertising hoardings cluttering the great views of the city – and so on. In his words, he wanted to 'keep it beautiful' for future generations. Yet, Dr Evelyn's prescient and wise words would be nothing without images to reinforce those words.

His home on 33 Bootham now has a Civic Trust plaque, commemorating his efforts for the preservation (and love) of the city. He was well known for his illustrated lectures; illustrated with old drawings he collected or the latest photographs.

Yet, Dr Evelyn did not possess a camera; for photography he relied on local photographer Thomas Hanstock. Dr Evelyn's York is also Thomas Hanstock's York. His beautiful images show a city through the Hanstock lens where well-dressed Edwardian ladies saunter across quiet roads, where only the occasional horse 'droppings' mar the smooth, well-laid stone setts and clean streets. Motor vehicles are infrequent, novel additions and new roads such as Crichton Avenue (1932) are seen as things of which to be proud. Hanstock lived in an age of rapid change, where horses and cyclists were giving way to trams, motor vehicles and gleaming new buildings and works and, after 1901, war memorials. His works cover the public and private; portraits and family groups – the bread and butter of the working photographer. He died in the dark days of the Second World War and worked right to the end with a spectacular series of views from a gasholder, affording a unique 360-degree panorama of York with leaden light and innumerable chimneys.

I am proud to be the first York-born chairman of YAYAS and trust you will enjoy the images that Hanstock has left our society. Some have not been seen since he clicked the shutter almost a century ago.

John R. Shaw BA (Hons), Chairman YAYAS

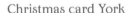

Christmas card York

❧ Introduction ❧

ON 7 OCTOBER 1842 THE FIRST general meeting of the Yorkshire Architectural Society (YAS) was held in Leeds. More than 300 people had expressed the opinion that the Society would fulfil an obvious need and were willing to join. That obvious need was to study the remains of ecclesiastical architecture, antiquities and design within the County of York and the improvement of the character of ecclesiastical edifices to be erected in the future. Despite these good intentions, over the next 60 years the activities and membership numbers of the Yorkshire Architectural Society steadily declined and by 1900 membership stood at only 27, of which 14 lived in the City of York.

In January 1891 Dr William Arthur Evelyn left a foggy London to start a new life as a GP in York. He spent the rest of his life studying the history of the city and amassing a collection of York iconography, ranging from seventeenth-century drawings to contemporary photographs.

Dr Evelyn joined the ailing YAS and was instrumental in the Society's rejuvenation, including a change of name to reflect the widening scope of the Society's aims. Recognising the prevailing interests of the majority of its members and potential new members, YAS changed its name and became the Yorkshire Architectural and York Archaeological Society. Today, more than 175 years after the inaugural meeting, YAYAS, as the Society is affectionately known and more easily pronounced, continues to pursue its aims of facilitating study of the county's heritage and safeguarding its future from inappropriate development.

Dr Evelyn remained an active member of YAYAS until his death in 1935. In July 1931 he handed over his collection of images to the City of York. He did in fact sell the collection to the city at a fraction of its true worth, refusing substantially higher offers, including one from Harvard University. It was Dr Evelyn's wish that the collection should stay in York. During his lifetime Dr Evelyn not only had the whole of his collection photographed but he also commissioned numerous photographs of the city as it existed in the first quarter of the twentieth century. This was no mean feat in the days

Dr Evelyn in 1914

when negatives consisted of chemically coated glass plates used in tripod-mounted wooden framed cameras. Over the years Dr Evelyn had built up a large collection of glass lantern slides, which he used in his many lectures, together with the associated glass plate negatives. In December 1934 Dr Evelyn, by this time suffering from poor health, donated this significant collection to YAYAS. YAYAS was charged with the safe keeping of the collection of over 3,000 images, which was to be made generally available to all for research and educational purposes.

This donation was the start of YAYAS' photographic collections, which is still to this day referred to as The Evelyn Collection. Over the ensuing years the collection has been added to with a number of other photographic collections given to YAYAS, all primarily focused on the City of York and its surrounding area. Pre-eminent among these gifts is a collection of plate negatives from the former York photography business of Thomas J. W. Hanstock.

In June 1998 The Hanstock Collection of glass plate negatives was given to YAYAS by Vanessa Ayres on the instructions of her late father, Peter Wilmott Hanstock. Peter Hanstock was a long-time member of YAYAS and the son of Thomas Joseph Wilmott and Florence Hanstock. It was Peter's express wish that his collection of photographic negatives of York and surrounding villages be freely conveyed to YAYAS and that 'these negatives are retained in York for perpetuity & not transferred to any other national photographic archive/collection situated outside York'. In addition to the collection of negatives, the Hanstock bequest also included a collection of glass plate negatives from an earlier York photographer, Joseph Duncan (1820 to 1895) one of the earliest photographers of the City of York.

Thomas Joseph Wilmott Hanstock was born in Doncaster on 23 February 1871. In 1898 he married Mary H. R. Black, moving to York in the same year. When he first arrived in York Hanstock worked as a joiner. In 1908 he started a professional photography business.

'Hanstock Thom. Joseph' first appears in *Kelly's Directory for York* in 1909. He is shown as a 'Photographer of 11 Clarence Street' which is recorded as both his business premises and his residence. The 1913 entry shows his business as 'Photographer Architectural work a speciality'. Sometime after the 1911 census, Thomas Hanstock and his wife Mary separated (although she continued to live locally until her death in 1945). The *Kelly's Directory* entries remain more or less unchanged until the 1938 edition after which publication was suspended for the duration of World War II. Publication recommenced with the 1949/50 edition, which shows the occupant of 11 Clarence Street as Hanstock T. J. However the 'Trade Photographers' entry in this edition lists Hanstock F., his second wife Florence, as the operator of the business. Thomas Joseph Wilmott Hanstock had in fact died in 1942. The final directory entry is in 1969 where the 'Trade Photographers' listing is: 11 Clarence St. Mrs F. A. The residential entry for 11 Clarence Street reads 'Hanstock Mrs. Florence A. Photographer'. The photography business of the Hanstock family had thus been active in the city for 60 years. The 1909 directory lists 15 professional photographers in York, the 1969 volume lists 11.

Peter Wilmott Hanstock, Thomas's son by his second wife Florence, was born on 2 March 1920. Peter worked with his father learning the skills needed to run a successful photographic business. Peter's main career was, however with the telephone communications department of the London and North Eastern Railway and latterly the Eastern Region of British Railways.

Notwithstanding his principal occupation as a railway engineer, Peter's interest in photography continued throughout his life. He was a competent painter and a practical engineer. His engineering skills were put to good use when he made specialist enlargers capable of producing prints from his father's half plate negatives, together with larger format negatives that he had collected from earlier photographers. He also used his artistic skills to restore prints made from damaged negatives in his collection. Peter Hanstock died in February 1995.

In June 1998 Peter Hanstock's daughter, Vanessa Ayres, contacted YAYAS to inform the Society that she had a Letter of Authority from her late father 'gratuitously conveying the HANSTOCK collection of photographic negatives of YORK & surrounding VILLAGES etc at present belonging to Mr P. W. Hanstock to THE YORKSHIRE ARCHITECTURAL & YORK ARCHAEOLOGICAL SOCIETY'. Peter Hanstock had been a prominent council member of the Society for many years and was close friends with fellow Council member Hugh Murray. It was a condition of the conveyance that Hugh was to have free access to and use of the collection at all times. The collection itself, consisting of over 160 boxes of glass plates of varying sizes was initially transferred to Hugh's home. It was later moved to join the Evelyn Collection and YAYAS archives held in the library of York Minster, where it can be found today.

As noted above, the *Kelly's Trade Directory for York* in 1913 lists T. J. Hanstock as 'Photographer, Architectural work a speciality' – all other directories just describe him as 'Photographer'. A trade label found in a box of original negatives details a much wider range of activities for the business, reading:

> T J Hanstock, Architectural & Commercial Photographer.
> 11 Clarence Street, York.
>
> Specialist in Architectural Photography, Landscapes, Groups, Instantaneous views, Enlarging, Picture Framing & c.

This box of negatives relates to an order from the Headmaster of Archbishop Holgate's Grammar School, P. J. Vinter. Mr Vinter was headmaster of AHGS between 1915 and 1937 so the trade label must therefore date to this period. The portraits of the Vinter family and others in the collection of pupils from the school giving a gymnastic display were taken outside the school and headmaster's house (page 120). This must have been a welcome commission for Hanstock as the school was then situated in Lord Mayor's Walk less than 200 yards from his premises at 11 Clarence Street.

One area of the business not specifically mentioned on this trade label is the production and publication of postcards, although it could be that this is covered under the somewhat enigmatic heading 'instantaneous views'. As is the case today, in the first half of the twenty-first century, York was one of the most visited cities in the land. Unlike today, visitors at the time were not armed with digital cameras and mobile phones. Back then postcards filled the dual role of providing keepsake pictures and keeping in contact with family and friends, when away from home. The selling and buying of postcards was big business with shops specialising in their sale. It was not unknown for a postcard sent in the morning to arrive at its destination that very afternoon. Postcards were the equivalent then of the now ubiquitous text message, Instagram, WhatsApp, Facebook and other social media.

J. T. Hanstock duly invested his photographic knowledge and expertise in the production of picture postcards relating to many of the most significant events in the city from around 1909 to just before the outbreak of World War II. He also produced postcard views of the city and surrounding villages, many of which are now highly prized by collectors. Today, unused, good condition postcards produced by Hanstock fetch considerable sums in the collectors' market.

Despite the vast number of photographs taken of York, few clear images of the outside of Hanstock's premises at 11 Clarence Street exist – no surprise given that this part of the city is not the most photogenic or picturesque. There have been a number of near misses though: one of the original negatives in the collection is a view of the corner of Gillygate and Lord Mayor's Walk with part of Clarence Street in the background.

Whole sections of shops were given over to stocks
of postcards in Edwardian days. This is Arthur's Postcard Depot
in Davygate in 1900

Hanstock's Victor Studio is situated on the corner of Clarence Street and
Union Terrace. The first-floor bay window visible immediately above the
lorry centre picture is the Hanstock premises. The lorry obscures the lower
floor bay. People living in the surrounding area in the 1950s recall this
window featuring displays of photographs and postcards. Another view by
a contemporary York-based photographer and postcard publisher William
Hayes, shows Clarence Street looking towards Gillygate. On the extreme
right-hand edge of the photograph you can just see the pavement entering
Union Terrace with the bay windows of Hanstock's Victor Studio at No 11
on the corner.

Although the first trade directory mention of Thomas Hanstock does not
appear until around 1909, he had more than a passing interest in photography before this. Thomas, as previously mentioned, was originally a joiner.
A note in a box of negatives written by Thomas's son Peter provides evidence
of this and reads '3 plates of Haxby Road School taken Dec. 1903 by T J W
Hanstock before school occupied by staff and pupils in 1904. TJWH worked
as a joiner foreman on this school' (see page 109).

It is clear from the many examples included in YAYAS' Hanstock

Clarence Street today. Hanstock's home and studio was where the trees are centre picture in what is now Clarence Street car park

Clarence Street about 1900, looking towards Gillygate, by York-based photographer and postcard publisher William Hayes. The bay-windowed house at the right-hand edge of the photograph is number 11, later to become Thomas Hanstock's home and studio

The studio backdrop, and below, the photographer's head clamp –
not the torture instrument you might think

collection that portraits formed a significant part of the business. Originals
exist for individuals, family groups,
group special occasions and, albeit rarely,
formal wedding photographs. Some of
these are taken on location and others in
the Victor Studio. Essential equipment
for a professional photographer's studio
at the time included a range of backdrops
and props. Due to the long exposure
times required, a clamping arrangement
to help sitters to remain still was also
essential. Photographs of some of his
studio equipment are included in the
Hanstock Collection.

Sadly, although the collection includes
many examples of his portrait work, it

The wedding of Edwin Ridsdale Tate to Mary Louisa Wray on 28th September 1916. Ridsdale Tate was a York-based architect and artist and was an associate of Dr. Evelyn and Thomas Hancock

does not feature any photographs of the man himself or of his family. Self-portraits clearly did not appeal and today's vogue for instant 'selfies' was still decades away. It was not until many years later that a picture appeared in The *York Press* of T. J. Hanstock sitting in a motorcycle sidecar. This print came from his granddaughter Mrs Joyce Hill.

This was not Hanstock's first encounter with a motor bike or indeed with the local press. On 23 July 1921 the *Driffield Times* reported on a number of cases recently heard at Norton Police Court. These included four individuals' summonses for riding motor cycles with the rear identification plate obscured. On this occasion Thomas Hanstock was able to put his professional skills to an unusual but effective use. To quote the report:

> Thos. Hanstock the first defendant created some amusement by stating that when the officer pulled him up he called to his assistant for his camera to take a photo. Before he could take it, the officer pulled down the frill of the cushion over the identification plate and said that was where the cushion was [at the time of the offence]. He handed the photographs to the Bench. P C Snowden questioned by the Bench said that was not a correct photograph as the cushion had been pulled down a little. Defendant denied this. Defendant said it was a shame the officer should be untruthful. The Chairman said it was a difficult case and they would dismiss the case on payment of costs.

The case against another of the defendants was also dismissed, the remaining two were less fortunate, being fined 10 shillings (50p) each. Clearly, even in 1921, it paid to always carry a camera with you.

Hanstock's Victoria Studio was situated less than a mile away from The York County Hospital in Monkgate. As part of his business, but

Thomas Hanstock in the motorbike side-car. Courtesy York Press

probably more for philanthropic rather than commercial reasons, Thomas was a frequent visitor to the hospital assisting the senior medical staff to take X-rays. The use of X-rays in medical imaging was still relatively new, having been discovered in 1895.

In addition to this, a brief profile of Thomas Hanstock in archives held by the Borthwick Institute at York University describes how he gave a demonstration to the Matron of York County Hospital outlining the potential of wireless broadcasting and its manifold benefits to hospital patients. In 1925–6 Hanstock was involved in the installation of a wireless system in the County Hospital, one of the first such systems in the country. Hospital radio had arrived. The collection includes a picture of a gentleman patient apparently enjoying wireless listening from the comfort of his hospital bed.

Local residents recall the business at 11 Clarence Street being run by an elderly lady up until 1968 by which time parts of Clarence Street and Union Terrace were earmarked for demolition. Florence Hanstock then closed the business and moved away.

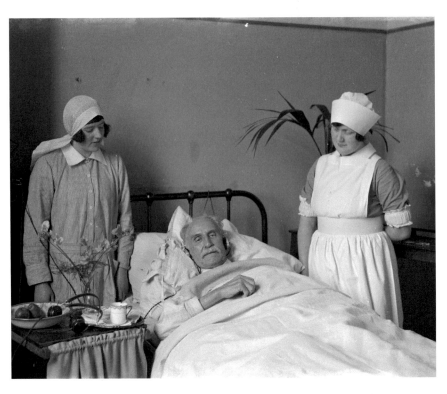

A patient enjoying some hospital radio as pioneered
by Thomas Hanstock

❧ Events & celebrations ❧

Y ORK, TO THIS DAY, COULD NEVER be accused of missing an opportunity
to celebrate. Here are just a few events which Hanstock snapped in the
early part of the twentieth century.

Military Sunday: presenting arms in Duncombe Place

An audience outside the Minster on Military Sunday

The ever popular Military Sunday was set up in 1885 by the then Dean, the Very Reverend Purey Cust, as a memorial to General Charles George Gordon (1833–85) killed at the Siege of Khartoum in 1885. The Sundays lasted until 1939 and were hugely popular with some people walking through the night to attend them.

The cap badge worn by the soldiers may be that of the King's Own (Royal Lancaster Regt) – First World War cap badge; the soldiers on the right may be Bantams.

The 1909 pageant was a dramatisation of York's history in seven episodes from 800 BCE to 1644 CE. With a cast of 2,500 this truly epic production involved 800 costume designs by forty different artists; 2,000 tracings were made and coloured – all based on information supplied by such authorities as the British Museum, Magdalen College, Oxford and Ampleforth College. The chorus comprised 220 singers.

The Mystery Plays had been bowdlerised (with scenes involving the Virgin Mary cut) and then completely suppressed in 1569; it was not until 1909 when this revival of sorts took place, performed in and around the

York Pageant 1909, showing Blake Street decked out for the occasion, complete with triumphal arch

York Pageant 1909, Museum Street

The York Pageant procession crossing a beautified Lendal Bridge

York Pageant

Museum Gardens. It included a parade of the banners of the York Guilds through the streets, accompanying a wagon representing the Nativity.

Later that year a selection of six plays was performed as a fund-raising venture for St Olave's Church. The York Pageant was never intended as a religious ceremony although it inevitably included religious episodes: these are inextricably wound up in any 'dramatic representation of the evolution of the old northern capital of Britain' (*The Book of the York Pageant 1909*).

The Romans in York

Eboracum was occupied by the Romans from AD 71 until AD 410 when they departed Britannia for good, leaving York to look after its own defence. In the beginning Quintus Petillius Cerialis led the IXth Hispana Legion north to subdue the Brigantes and established a garrison here. Strategically York was of major significance, being of considerable military importance and a major communications centre. The Colonia covered sixty acres and the walls were twenty feet high and four feet thick in parts. The Praetorium is under the Minster, there is quite possibly an amphitheatre and temple and

York Pageant: Romans in a Roman city

York Pageant: sedans for hire

York Pageant ~ looking like early auditions for
'The Handmaid's Tale'!

18

a basilica under Micklegate, baths on the banks of the Ouse, a sewerage system in Bishophill, a VIth Victrix Legion column opposite the Minster and a statue of Constantine nearby to celebrate his being proclaimed Emperor here in 306 on the death of his father, the Emperor Constantius Chlorus in York, and his conversion to Christianity, probably in 312. Septimius Severus, Rome's first black emperor, lived in York between 208 and 211; his sons, Caracalla and Geta, were declared co-Emperors in 198 and 209. Severus died in York in 211 and received a spectacular funeral in the city, but not before he had declared York to be the capital of Britannia Inferior. Hadrian visited too in the second century.

A character from the 1909 York Pageant

Another scene from the 1909 York Pageant

The 1909 Pageant was produced as a dramatic representation of the city's history in seven episodes from 800 BC to AD 1644. Everything – every costume, every banner, every suit of armour – was designed and produced by the people of York over two years. More than 2,500 actors and dancers took part, with soldiers from the 2nd Yorkshire Regiment and the 5th Lancers, together with 103 horses, joining in as well.

The Grand Yorkshire Gala

Going up in a tethered hot air balloon was a regular feature at the annual Grand Yorkshire Gala held in the grounds of Bootham Park Hospital (which became known as Gala Fields) from 1858 to 1923. Other attractions included military bands, roundabouts, a helter-skelter: Holdsworth's Alpine Glassade – 'Why go to Switzerland?' 'Ladies Specially Invited'; evening firework displays, acrobatics, juggling and shooting galleries. So popular was it that it became a three-day event and seriously depressed attendances

The Grand Yorkshire Gala. Note the tethered balloon
in the background

at York races when they coincided. The Gala moved to Fulford in 1924 and
then to the Knavesmire.

Thomas Hanstock was a regular visitor to The Great Yorkshire Gala in
the early 1900s. This event was attended by hundreds of Yorkshire folk, some
of whom had a more enjoyable time than others. In June 1911 Thomas and
his camera were on hand to record what the *Ripon and Richmond Chronicle*
headlined as 'Passengers' Terrifying Adventure' – a 'mishap' (the *Chronicle's*
word) occurred when a cable snapped as one balloon was being hauled to
the ground.

The balloon, carrying the pilot and nine passengers (including two ladies
and three of the Gala's entertainers) broke free, reaching a height of several
hundred feet.

Pursued by the intrepid Major T. N. Lindberg on a bicycle, the balloon
floated on for some 11 miles coming to rest in a tree near Elvington, having
been in the air for nearly an hour. The tireless Major Lindberg caught up
with the balloon and was able to phone back to the Gala that the passengers
had suffered only minor scratches and bruises. Phew!

Captain P. Liwery, breakaway balloon pilot: would you trust this man?

The local press were quick to report the incident

The balloon at various stages of take-off. Note the ballast bags in the image above

A well-attended opening ceremony for a new bandstand on the Knavesmire racecourse, with the Lord Mayor and Sheriff of the city much in evidence. A large crowd is standing behind the ropes watching the proceedings

Above: seats available … and below: … not any more

In June 1932 the Corporation opened a new bridge over the railway line to Scarborough. The new bridge replaced an earlier level crossing giving a better connection to the new housing estate on Burton Stone Lane with Wigginton Road and the Rowntree factory. Thomas Hanstock photographed the previous crossing, the bridge under construction and a train passing under the new bridge with a young train spotter looking on. He is probably Thomas's son Peter who would contribute to the photography business in later life.

Burton Stone crossing

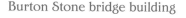
Burton Stone bridge building

The completed
Burton Stone bridge

A new pavilion was opened in Clarence Gardens on 16 July 1913. Celebrating the event are members of the Clarence Gardens Bowling Club and a number of veterans who regularly used the gardens. Everyone attending was immaculately turned out, sporting various styles of natty headwear. The central figure in the image below helpfully holds a board clearly showing the event and date. It appears no ladies were invited to the official celebrations

The Coronation of King George V was on 22 June 1911.
A large celebratory party took place in Bootham Park, as the
images on this page show. Hundreds of children attended, mainly
from the many church groups in the city at the time
('St Patrick Pray For Us')

The steam-driven carousel in the image above is interestingly
promoted as the 'Grand Stud of Racers'

York celebrated the coronation of King George V in a number of different
ways. Electric illuminations were installed on the Mansion House, all four
of York's famous bars and on a number of the city's trams.

Left and opposite page:
some of the illuminated
installations around
the city to celebrate the
coronation of George V

Yorkshire's first ever aviation meeting was held on Doncaster Race Course in 1909. By 1913 York's Knavesmire was a regular stopping off and refuelling point for a series of air races.

York Air Races

Avro number 8 seen here in the foreground has taken part in the 'War of the Roses' race in October 1913. Immediately behind is the race winner, a Blackburn Monoplane piloted by Mr F. P. Raynham. Many of these races were organised by the *Daily Mail* hence the underwing advertising, clearly visible from the ground. In 1911 the *Mail* arranged this Circuit of Britain Race with a first prize of £10,000, a substantial sum in 1911.

Underwing 'DAILY MAIL' advertising

Opening York Aerodrome, 4 July 1936

After speeches the 26th Army Co-operation squadron RAF flew over the aerodrome and the city. This was followed by an air display which featured ten different aircraft including a British Empire Display Team. The Civic Party, which included Cllr. A. G. Watson, Chairman of the Parks Committee, who was responsible for the operation of the aerodrome, was invited to take an inaugural flight in a Croydon Monospar, a large (for its day) passenger machine piloted by Lord Semphill. The General Aircraft Monospar was a 1930s British family of touring and utility aircraft built by General Aircraft Ltd.

The General Aircraft Croydon Monospar at the opening of
York Aerodrome in 1936

York City Aerodrome opened in 1936, five years after Airspeed Ltd was established in York in Piccadilly Bus Garage, designing aeroplanes and gliders. The company was run by Nevil Shute, later to become a bestselling author. Later, Yorkshire Aviation Services operated from Clifton Moor offering flying lessons and an air taxi service; it became an RAF base during World War II.

The Duke and Duchess of York leaving after a 1925 visit to the
Mansion House to unveil a bronze plaque given to the city by
the City of New York

The opening of each season of the Assizes in York was marked with due
ceremony. Hanstock photographed the events in 1911 including the Civic
Party, judges and magistrates visiting the Minster for the Assizes Sunday
sermon, breakfasting in the Mansion House and holding a formal opening
ceremony in the Guildhall.

York Assizes, 1911

Proclamation of George V

George V was proclaimed King on 10 May 1920 from a number of strategic locations throughout the City including the steps of the Mansion House and outside the east end of All Saints Pavement. The proclamation was read by the town Clerk Henry Craven in the presence of The Lord Mayor James Birch and Sheriff William Foster-Todd.

At 3 p.m. on Monday 20 February 1911 the Lord Mayor of York Alderman T. Carter unveiled a statue to William Etty R.A. (1787–1849). The statue stands proudly outside York City Art Gallery, the home of many of his, often controversial and to some, shocking paintings. Etty founded the York School of Design in 1842, later the York School of Art. He first exhibited at the Royal Academy in 1811, becoming an Academician in 1828.

In 1905 Dr W. A. Evelyn (1860–1935) organized an exhibition in York City Art Gallery – *York Views and Worthies* – comprising images of York. He started his famous series of lectures in 1909 and in 1934 he sold his huge collection of pictures to the city for the knocked-down price of £3,000 to be held in the gallery, the money having been raised by public subscription and not from the city's coffers. A fervent defender of the city's heritage and member of York Architectural and York Archaeological Society (YAYAS), Dr Evelyn campaigned tirelessly against the destruction or ruination of many of York's finest sights. The Evelyn Collection is accessible through YAYAS, www.yayas.free-online.co.uk We have much to thank him for when it comes to the surviving walls, bars and buildings of York. His sonorous letter to the city's official vandals resonates to this day:

> Beware how you destroy your antiquities, guard them with religious care! They are what give you a decided character and superiority over other provincial cities. You have lost much, take care of what remains.

A before and after sequence of the unveiling of the
William Etty statue in 1911

The Etty view

He is buried in St Olave's, Marygate. This church is named after the patron Saint of Norway, St Olaf.

The Etty statue is the work of York's leading sculptor and carver George Walker Milburn. The statue gazes directly towards the opening in the city walls (the walls he did much to save) adjacent to Bootham Bar where Milburn had his work premises from 1885 to 1941. 'G. W. Milburn' can just be made out on the signboard above the archway entrance to his yard.

A temporary building was erected in the grounds of Bootham Park Hospital for the first Yorkshire Fine Art and Industrial Exhibition. Made entirely from wood and glass the front was decorated with royal coats of arms and those of the patrons.

The Italianate building which today houses the gallery opened its doors to the public in 1879 for the second exhibition, inspired by the Great Exhibition in London of 1851. The York exhibition attracted more than half a million visitors and made a profit of £12,000. In 1892 it became the City Art Gallery. The building continued in use from 1880 as the Yorkshire Fine Art and Industrial Institution until 1892 when it was purchased by the City

Council. The original building had a 'Great Exhibition Hall' at the rear with room for 2,000 people. This was a venue for boxing and cock fighting as well as exhibitions; it was damaged by bombs during WWII and demolished in 1942.

The Gallery's collection was initiated in 1882 when a retired horse dealer from Poppleton, John Burn, was persuaded to leave his collection of paintings to the city rather than to his first choice, the National Gallery. Apart from numerous paintings of York and its buildings there are many works by William Etty. Every year between 1950 and 1962 an artist was paid £50 to produce a picture of York: L. S. Lowry's painting of Clifford's Tower is one of the results.

York Minster bells

The twelve bells of York Minster before rehanging, after a major restoration by John Warner & Sons Ltd of The Spitalfields Bell Foundry in March 1914. The restored bells returned by steamer to Hull and on to York by rail. A further restoration was needed as early as 1924, this time being carried out by John Taylors of Loughborough

❧ Historic buildings ❧

THE ORIGINAL NAME FOR THE ARCHBISHOP'S Palace was Thorpe, as given in *Domesday*, then Thorpe-on-Ouse in 1194; in 1275 we find Biscupthorpe. In 1202 the monks of St Andrew's at Fishergate built the first church here and the name changed to Andrewthorpe, Thorpe St Andrew or St Andrewthorpe; this changed to Bishopthorpe in the thirteenth century when Archbishop Walter de Grey bought the manor house and presented it to the Dean and Chapter of York Minster. Bishopthorpe Palace was thus born; it has been the residence of the Archbishop of York ever since. In 1323 a truce was signed here between Edward II and Robert the Bruce after the Battle of Bannockburn. Archbishop Drummond's renovation of the Palace in 1763 produced the Strawberry Hill Gothic west front and gatehouse. In 1832 Reform Bill rioters tried to overrun the Palace, incensed by Archbishop Harcourt's lack of support.

One of York's more colourful archbishops was Lancelot Blackburne. Blackburne died in 1743; he was Archbishop of York from 1724 until his death before which he did time as a paid spy of Charles II in 1681, and as a pirate in the Caribbean in the 1680s. He reputedly drank ale and smoked a pipe during confirmations, behaviour typical of the man and described as follows: 'His behaviour was seldom of a standard to be expected of an archbishop … in many respects it was seldom of a standard to be expected of a pirate'.

Between 1480 and 1500 Archbishop Rotherham added the North Wing to the palace; between 1761 and 1769 Archbishop Drummond appointed John Carr to design the Gothic stable block and gatehouse. In 1766–9 the front of the palace was built, providing a new entrance hall and drawing

Facing page: two wonderful pictures of the Archbishop's Palace in Bishopthorpe. The first shows vintage motorcars and chauffeurs while the second depicts two ladies outside waiting for someone to arrive

The palace from the river

room. There is also a brewhouse and brewster's cottage. This description captures the grandeur and antiquity of the palace well:

> The Great Hall rebuilt in the 17th century but based on that of the original 13th century room has rich plasterwork in the ceiling and the deep frieze. The windows have coats of arms of various Archbishops in colourful stained glass. Archbishop Richard Scrope was tried for treason here in the Great Hall in 1405 before Henry IV. Having been found guilty he was beheaded and was the only Archbishop in England ever to be executed. The Chapel, although having been restored by Archbishop Maclagan in 1891, retains much of its original fabric from 1241, in particular the walls and lancet windows. The attractive blue ceiling was inserted in Archbishop Vernon Harcourt's time to allow rooms to be built above. (Source: Michael Ford http://www.britannia.com/history/chouses/bpthorpe.html.)

Clifford's Tower

Originally called the King's Tower, or, if you like, the 'Minced Pie'. From 1596 it became known as Clifford's Tower, named after Francis Clifford, Earl of Cumberland, who restored it for use as a garrison after it had been partly dismantled by Robert Redhead in 1592. An alternative etymology comes from Roger de Clifford whose body was hung there in chains in 1322.

Built in wood by William the Conqueror when he visited to establish his northern HQ in 1190, it was burnt down after 150 terrified York Jews sought sanctuary here from an anti-Semitic mob; faced with the choice of being killed or forced baptism, many committed suicide; 150 others were slaughtered. It was rebuilt in stone by King John and Henry III as a quadrilobate between 1245 and 1259 as a self-contained stronghold and royal residence,

Inside Clifford's Tower. Established as one of two York castles by William I, it was rebuilt by Henry III in 1260 as part of the city's defences. The Stone Bar walls shown here replaced wooden pallisades. Clifford's Tower stands near the oval patch of grass known as the 'Eye of the Ridings'

The Eye of the Ridings

housing the kingdom's Treasury in the fourteenth century. Robert Aske, one of the prime movers in the Pilgrimage of Grace, was hanged here on 12 July 1537. On 23 April 1684 the roof was blown off during an over-enthusiastic seven gun salute. Deer grazed around the tower for many years; it became part of the prison in 1825. The motte is forty-eight foot high and the tower itself thirty-three feet. The moat was fed by a diversion from the Ouse.

Highwayman Dick Turpin, also known as John Palmer, was hanged (somewhat fittingly) on the Knavesmire in 1739, for horse stealing – 'a crime worthy of death'. Turpin spent his last six months in the Debtors' Prison, which was built in 1701–5. Turpin had many visitors: his jailer is said to have earned £100 from selling drinks to Turpin and his guests; Turpin bought a new frock coat and shoes and hired five mourners for £3 10s. for the occasion.

A report in the *Gentleman's Magazine* for 7 April 1739 notes Turpin's arrogance:

> Turpin behaved in an undaunted manner; as he mounted the ladder, feeling his right leg tremble, he spoke a few words to the topsman, then threw himself off, and expir'd in five minutes.

The short drop method of hanging meant that those executed were killed by slow strangulation: Turpin was left hanging until late afternoon, before being cut down and taken to the Blue Boar Inn in Castlegate. Turpin's grave

in St George's churchyard was dug particularly deep to deter body snatchers; to no avail: the corpse was exhumed and found later at the back of Stonegate in a surgeon's garden. Before reburial the coffin was filled with lime.

York Prison buildings

These were built in 1825 along Tower Street and demolished in the 1930s; they enclosed the Debtor's Prison and the Female Prison – both now occupied by the Castle Museum which has a section devoted, appropriately, to prison life. Daniel Defoe, with the distinct advantage of seeing things from the outside, admired the prison, describing it as 'the most stately and complete of any in the whole kingdom, if not in Europe'. The cells in which prisoners like Dick Turpin spent their last days before execution can be visited today as part of the museum (with impunity). A World War I tank stood sentinel in Tower Gardens for many years as a memorial to the Great War – before it was melted down in World War II for scrap.

York Castle Museum opened in 1938 and is one of Britain's leading museums of everyday life. It is famous for its Victorian street, Kirkgate, named after the museum's founder, Dr John Lamplugh Kirk, a Pickering doctor who collected everyday objects, his 'bygones', and for whom the Museum was converted from the Women's Prison as somewhere to keep them safe for future generations.

External and internal views of York Prison, built in 1825 and
demolished in 1935

York Prison walls

York Prison and the Foss

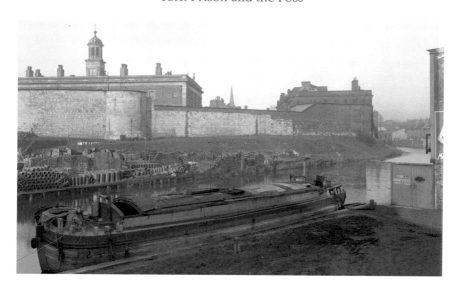

An unusual shot of York's city walls, showing Robin Hood's Tower

Robin Hood's Tower

The tower is situated on the walls between Bootham and Monk Bar, and is named probably for no other reason, like the Robin Hood pub in Castlegate, than that Robin Hood and what he stood for was 'a good thing'. The existing tower is an 1899 replacement. The walls were built in the thirteenth and fourteenth century on a rampart dating from the ninth and eleventh centuries. They survive for the best part of their two miles plus length as do the four Bars and thirty-seven internal towers. Four of the six posterns and nine other towers are lost or have been rebuilt. The walls for the most part are six foot wide and thirteen foot high. They were breached in two places in the 1840s to allow access to York's second railway station and to a goods depot known as the Sack Warehouse.

Wilkie Collins (1824–89) was a frequent visitor; he set his 1862 novel, *No Name*, in the city describing a walk along the walls by Captain Wragge as

> one of the most striking scenes which England can show … the majestic west front of York Minster soared over the city and caught the last brightest light of heaven on the summits of its lofty towers.

The Residence, York Minster

The Old Residence

The Old Residence was at the south-east corner of the minster, probably built in the early eighteenth century to house canons during their period of residence. The New Residence in Dean's Park, a two-storey stone house with attics, was built in 1824. The Old Residence was later occupied by the headmaster of St Peter's School, the Chapter Clerk, the registrar, and others. In 1959 it was used by the junior school of the York College for Girls. The New Residence was used by the chapter until 1920 when a new statute enabled canons in residence to live in other houses. Today, the Dean and the Residentiary Canons are required to live in the vicinity of the Minster, and take turns being 'in residence'. They are present at morning and evening prayer for the week. The Canon in Residence is on hand to meet pastoral needs, and may be required to chair committees or deputise for the Dean.

York city walls, and the Station Hotel

The Station Hotel

The arch was punched through the city walls in 1846 to give access to York's second station. A sumptuous hotel was part of the plan when the new station was built, although the hotel did not open until 1878. It was given the name Royal York Hotel, as this is where it was assumed Victoria would usually alight for lunch *en route* to Balmoral.

Nothing if not grand and elegant, its five storeys offered 100 stylish bedrooms at fourteen shillings a night. Each of the rooms had its own coal fire. Three entrances allowed access: the town entrance, the garden entrance and the tiled octagonal entrance – used by patrons arriving by train. The garden, or west, entrance, was lost when the twenty-seven room west wing extension was built; this took the name 'Klondyke' as this was the year of the Gold Rush. A new garden entrance was built in 1939. The original electric doorbell survives with its panel of buzzers and discs by the porter's desk. The coffee room with its splendid views of the river is now the restaurant while the east wing boasted a smoke-room and a billiard room with its magnificent ceramic tiles. The wooden reading racks in what was the oak-paneled reading room in the Klondyke Wing have survived.

In 1841 what is known as the Old Railway Station was opened within the city walls, designed by the celebrated York architect G. T. Andrews. The site was once the home of a Dominican friary and later of the spectacular nursery gardens of James and Thomas Backhouse – known nationally as the Kew of the North. Lady Hewley's Hospital and the 1814 House of Correction were demolished to make way.

Opening day, 4 January 1841, was a public holiday in York with church and Minster bells ringing out and huge crowds celebrating the event. Original plans included a booking office facing Tanner Row (cost £7,900), a refreshment room, and a train shed. The large shed (300 by 100 feet) was of iron and glass construction supported by cast-iron columns and was unique at the time. The Italianate facade, facing Tanner Row, was 180 feet long; access between the platforms came at the head of the tracks – one of the earliest stations in the world with such a facility. The King of Saxony and Charles Dickens were amongst travellers arriving here. The King visited York in 1844 with Carl Gustav Carus, his physician, who left a detailed account of the stay.

St Helen's Square and church

The square was purchased from St Helen's churchyard in 1703 to allow the gentry easier carriage access to the Assembly Rooms, thus avoiding the messy and baneful graveyard. The church was actually in the process of being demolished in 1551 before it was reprieved and rebuilt. The 1876 lantern

St Helen's Square and church

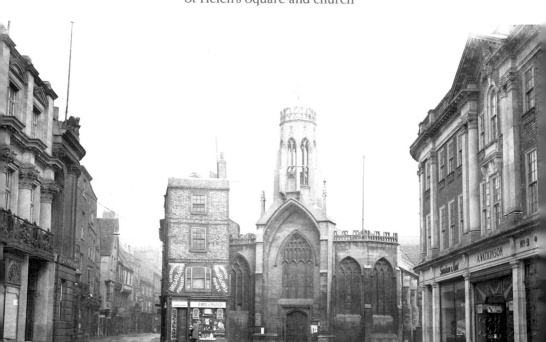

tower replaced a steeple. The maiden Davyes sisters, Barbara and Elizabeth, were buried here, both ninety-eight, and witnesses to seven monarchs from Charles II to George III. Their nephew, Theophylus Davyes Garencières, was related to the eminent French physician Theophylus Garencières (d. 1680). Davyes died of yellow fever in St Domingo in 1797. The Savings Bank was built in 1829, the Yorkshire Insurance Building in 1840. This shot was taken before Bettys took over the corner site on the right – then a furniture warehouse. Terry's is on the left.

The Knavesmire and Alicia Meynell

York Races has been a major summer event in the city for hundreds of years. Held at the Knavesmire, the races are a significant event in the nation's racing calendar. A major improvement scheme, launched in 1962, led to the opening of the magnificent six-tier grandstand in 1965.

Horse races have been run at York since the reign of Roman Emperor Septimius Severus (r. AD 193–AD 211). In 1607, racing is known to have taken place on the frozen river Ouse, between Micklegate Tower and Skeldergate Postern. The first records of a race meeting are from 1709, when efforts were made to improve the flood-prone course at Clifton Ings; all to no avail so in 1730 racing moved to Knavesmire, where today's course remains. York architect, John Carr, designed and built the first Grandstand in 1754.

Alicia Meynell was the first woman jockey to compete in a horse race against men, at the Knavesmire in 1755 when she rode 'Vingarella' side-saddle. Victory, though, had to wait until the following year when she won on 'Louisa', again at the Knavesmire.

The Knavesmire

The Knavesmire

At one August meeting in the 1960s, special efforts appear to have been made to improve the catering: prodigious quantities of beef, pork and lamb were loaded into the County Stand, along with 400 grouse, 350 chickens, 100 Norfolk ducklings, 5000 pounds of Scotch salmon, 500 dover soles, 400 lobsters and fifty pounds of smoked salmon.

The racecourse stand from the rear

Portcullises in York

Portcullises survive in the four main Bars of York, however only that at Monk Bar retains its full machinery and is capable of being lowered. The Hanstock collection includes these rare photographs of Monk Bar's portcullis in the lowered position dated 3 March 1914. This was the first time the portcullis had been lowered in 300 years. The sign on the building immediately to the left of the Bar identifies it as 'The Central Registry Office for Servants' and the adjacent shop appears to be selling picture posts cards.

Monk Bar portcullis in the lowered position

A closer view of Monk Bar portcullis in the lowered position

Kings Edwin and Edward VII

The much-photographed choir screen in York minster famously contains the statues of 15 Kings of England. Hanstock produced postcards of statues of two Kings not included in the screen, the seventh-century King Edwin, who is said to have been married on the site of the present minster, and the twentieth-century King Edward VII.

Statue of King Edward VII

Statue of King Edwin

St William's College

Originally the House of the Prior of Hexham it is named after Archbishop William Fitzherbert (St William) and built in 1465 by order of Warwick the Kingmaker. The college was home to the Minster's Chantry: twenty-three chantry priests of the Liberty of Saint Peter and their provost. By 1547 the priests were subletting to laymen and by 1550 the building had passed completely into lay hands.

The priests in Bedern Chapel over the way off Goodramgate had been indulging in 'colourful nocturnal habits' and were re-housed in St William's College so that their behaviour could be monitored more closely. One incident involved one of the cathedral freelances hitting a man over the head with (the blunt end of) an axe.

Charles I established his propaganda Royal printing house here during the Civil War and it was used as the Royal Mint at one time. The current central doors were made by Robert Thompson of Kilburn: his signature mouse can be seen on the right hand door.

Over the next 350 years the neglected building deteriorated into a series of tenanted properties. In 1899 the whole of the College was bought by Frank Green – a prosperous, if eccentric, West Riding industrialist for £1,500. Green then offered the College to The York Diocesan Trust for the same sum, provided the Trust undertook a sympathetic restoration. The cost

St William's College

The restoration of St William's College

St William's College, frontpost repair

of the restoration was estimated at £6,500. Today St William's ownership has gone full circle and it is now in the care of the Dean and Chapter of York.

Charles I set up his printing press in 1642 in Sir Henry Jenkins' house in St William's College. The royal presses rolled from March to August that year and turned out seventy-four documents including Charles' *Counsell of Warre*.

A rental document of 1845 tells us that annual rents are 32*s.* for five tenements, three cottages (2*s.* each) and one messuage (2*s.* 4*d.*). From 1680 to 1761 the cottages were variously occupied by a painter, joiner, translator, cordwainer. They were nearly demolished in 1912 to make way for the tramline to Heworth.

Re-opening of St William's College

Lendal Tower

The tower sits adjacent to Lendal Bridge. Necessitated by the need for access to the new railway, Lendal Bridge was opened in 1863 to replace the ferry

Lendal Tower

which plied between the Lendal and Barker Towers. Jon Leeman was the last ferryman – he received £15 and a horse and cart in redundancy compensation. The arrival of the railways had exerted considerable pressure on the ferry service and after considerable argument between the Corporation of York and the railway companies the York Improvement Act was passed in 1860 to allow construction of the first Lendal Bridge. It was designed by the unfortunately named William Dredge.

Tragically, because the bridge collapsed during construction, killing five men, it was replaced by the present bridge, designed by Thomas Page who was responsible also for Skeldergate Bridge in York and Westminster Bridge. Lendal Bridge displays the resplendent V&A insignia (honouring Queen Victoria and Prince Albert) and the crossed keys of St Peter symbolizing the Minster, with the Guildhall in the background. The remnants of Dredge's bridge were dredged up from the river and sold to Scarborough Council who used the remnants in the construction of Valley Bridge.

In 1677 Lendal Tower was leased for 500 years to the York Waterworks Company for two peppercorns (a peppercorn rent) and provided York's water supply until 1836 when the dedicated red brick engine house was built. The tower was put on the market for £650,000 in 2001 and sold as a private residence. The peppercorn rent is payable annually until 2177.

Monk Bar and the Bar Convent

The Bar Convent is the oldest lived-in convent in England. It was established as a school for Catholic girls in 1686 by Frances Bedingfield, an early member of Mary Ward's Institute, in response to Sir Thomas Gascoigne's demand: 'We must have a school for our daughters'. Sir Thomas, a local Catholic landowner, provided £450 to set up a boarding school; this was followed in 1699 by a free day school.

Frances Bedingfield had been imprisoned in Ousebridge Gaol for her religious beliefs. For Catholics the seventeenth century was often a time of persecution and the Bar Convent was very much a clandestine community. Known as the 'Ladies at the Bar' the sisters wore plain grey day dresses rather than habits to avoid raising suspicion. The community suffered great poverty, persecution and imprisonment – not just for their faith but also for teaching that faith. However, it survived, and in 1727 was joined by Elizabeth Stansfield and Ann Aspinal who paid off the community's debts and in the 1760s demolished the original house to replace it with the fine Georgian house and integral chapel on the site today. April 1769 saw the first Mass to be held in the beautiful new chapel, with its magnificent, but externally unobtrusive, neo-classical dome concealed beneath a pitched slate roof. Apart

Monk Bar and the Bar Convent: The Windmill pub is on the left, the Punch Bowl on the right, with Micklegate Bar in the centre. To the immediate right is the Bar Convent

from the discreet dome, the building has many other integral features which betray the secret nature of its activities. The chapel is situated in the centre of the building so that it cannot be seen from the street; its plain windows reveal nothing of its ecclesiastical nature and there are no fewer than eight exits, providing escape routes for the congregation in the event of a raid. There is also a priest hole which can still be seen today. The nuns who still live there belong to the Congregation of Jesus which was founded by Mary Ward (1585–1645).

The raids on York, Norwich, Bath, Canterbury and Exeter became known as the Baedeker raids because Goring's staff allegedly used the famous travel guide to select their *Vergeltungsangriffe* (retaliatory) targets – namely 3-star English cities – in retaliation for the RAF destruction of Lubeck and Rostock. On 28 April 1942 seventy German bombers, largely unopposed, bombed York for two hours: eighty-six people died including fourteen children, and ninety-eight were seriously injured (not including undisclosed army and RAF fatalities). 9500 houses (30 per cent of the city's stock) were damaged or destroyed leaving 2000 people homeless. The Guildhall and St Martin le Grand Church were badly damaged. The Bar Convent School collapsed killing five nuns including the headmistress, Mother Vincent. The following day the *Daily Mail* reported:

> The gates of York still stand high, like the spirit of its people who, after nearly two hours of intense bombing and machine-gunning, were clearing up today.

There is a plaque on York Railway Station in honour of Station Foreman William Milner who died in the raid while entering a burning building to get medical supplies. His body was found still holding the box; he was posthumously awarded the King's Commendation for Gallantry.

York Theatre Royal

The first theatre was built nearby on tennis courts in Minster Yard in 1734 by Thomas Keregan. In 1744 his widow built The New Theatre here on what was the city's Mint, itself built on the site of St Leonard's Hospital. In 1765 it was rebuilt by Joseph Baker and enlarged to seat 550, 'by far the

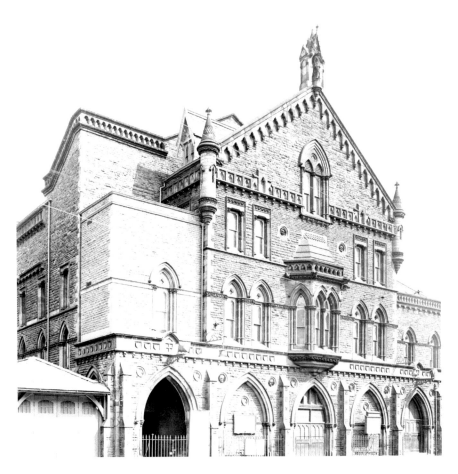

York Theatre Royal

most spacious in Great Britain, Drury Lane and Covent garden excepted', according to the *York Courant*. Access to the site of the Mint can still be gained from the back of the main stage. At this time the theatre was illegal and it was not until a Royal Patent was granted in 1769 and the theatre was renamed the Theatre Royal that this status changed. Gas lighting came in 1824 and in 1835 a new frontage was built facing onto the newly-created St Leonard's Place. This was removed to Fulford Road in 1880 and replaced with a new facade.

York Theatre Royal was the venue in 1853 for a concert by Miss Greenfield, a black, former slave girl; reviews in the *Yorkshire Gazette* were very favourable.

In 1866 we heard that 'Blind Tom is Coming! Blind Tom, the Inexplicable Phenomenon' who had recently wowed audiences at the St James's and Egyptian Halls in London (*York Herald*, 20 October). He too was an ex slave and a protégé of Charles Dickens who counted him as a 'valued friend'. Tom was a 'make weight' thrown into the deal when his mother was bought by a tobacco-planter: 'a lump of black flesh born blind, and with the vacant grin of idiocy'. Notwithstanding, he turned out to be a gifted pianist and a success on the novelty and trick circuit: for example,

> his most confusing feat was to play one air with his left hand, another with his right in a different key, whilst he sang a third tune in a different key again … experts such as the Head of Music at Edinburgh testified to his accuracy.

The 'encore' had its premiere in York, at the Theatre Royal in 1791 after a performance of the 'Conjuror's Song' in which a leg of lamb, a cake and a lawyer in a sack were conjured up. The audience enjoyed this so much that they demanded to see it again – a somewhat difficult request. Performers and orchestra left the stage amid a salvo of candles and candlesticks: the audience was only placated when the orchestra returned to play the song again.

The Ainsty Hotel

✍ Industry & public service ✍

YORK, BECAUSE OF ITS CLOTH TRADE and the ancillary industries associated with it in the fourteenth century, was described as 'the foremost industrial town in the North of England.' In 1384 there were 800 weavers in the city. This was short-lived though, and the trade in cloth declined to such a degree that a visitor to the city in the seventeenth century, Thomas Fuller, remarked: 'the foreign trade is like their river … low and flat.' Francis Drake records in his *Eboracum: or the History and Antiquities of the City of York,* that York in the eighteenth century had precious little industry and the only real commercial activity was butter exports, corn and wine trading. Daniel Defoe, in *A Tour Through the Whole Island of Great Britain* at first disagrees, describing 'considerable trade' with France, Norway and Portugal, and then, in contradiction, agrees: 'here is no trade … except such as depends upon the confluence of the gentry.' This industrial lethargy was due to some extent both to the high price of coal which had to be shipped from the coalfields of the West Riding, and to the restrictive, exclusive attitude of the local Merchant Adventurers and their insistence that all traders had to be Freemen of the City up until 1827. The railway and confectionery industries were soon to change the industrial landscape.

The Ainsty Hotel

The pub, in Boroughbridge Road, takes its name from the The Wapentake of Ainsty. It is in the roadhouse-style, built by York brewer J. J. Hunt of Spurriergate in 1930 to serve developments along the proposed ring road, which never materialised.

A wapentake is a subdivision of a county and is more or less the northern equivalent of a Hundred. The Wapentake of Ainsty, taking in thirty-five townships, is first recorded in the Domesday Book of 1086 (as Ainestig), when it was a wapentake of the West Riding of Yorkshire. It lay largely to the west of the city of York between the Rivers Ouse, Wharfe and Nidd and was named after Ainsty Cliff near Bilborough. The boundaries of the city parishes were first accurately surveyed by a Captain Tucker for the Ordnance Survey between 1846 and 1851 and marked on a large-scale plan published in 1852.

The Half Moon Inn

Another Hunt house which was in Blake Street from 1783, where McDonalds is now. There was another Half Moon in Jewbury and one in Trinity Lane, there was one in Strensall and there is one in Newton-on-Derwent. The pub's name may reflect the old tradition where large houses (including those owned by the Church) were often open to travellers for food and drink; signs such as a half moon would have indicated that the (public) house was a place of refreshment.

John J. Hunt Ltd, the Ebor Brewery in Aldwark, was founded by Joseph Hunt in 1834. Malting was its initial prime business – a new 25-quarter malting had been erected in 1860. It was only from 1890 that Hunt began to acquire public houses. The brewery was acquired with its 230 houses by J. W. Cameron & Co. Ltd. of West Hartlepool in 1953, including those of subsidiary Scarborough & Whitby Breweries Ltd. Brewing ended in 1956 and the site was demolished in 1972.

Some former John J. Hunt pubs include the Golden Lion Hotel, St Sampson's Square, Bell Hotel, Micklegate, Haymarket, Peasholme Green, Garrick's Head, Low Petergate, Alexandra, Market Street, Yorkshireman, Coppergate, Board Inn, Pavement, Londesborough Hotel, Low Petergate, St Peter's Vaults, Walmgate, Sportsman, Hungate, yet another Whig Punch Bowl, Lowther Street, Lamb Inn, Tanner Row, Magpie & Stump, Penley's Grove Street, Greyhound, Spurriergate, Fox Inn, Low Petergate, Newcastle Inn, North Street, Bumper Castle Inn, Wigginton Road, Knavesmire Hotel, Albemarle Road, Edinburgh Arms, Fishergate, and the races related Old Ebor, Nunnery Lane, Turf Tavern, Davygate, Saddle Hotel, York Road, Fulford.

Aldwark was less than ideal for such a business so a site for new offices and stores was acquired in Pavement. In June 1897, Hunt bought Brett Brothers' brewery, together with 15 licensed houses, for £74,000. Brett Brothers, operated from City Brewery, Church Lane, Low Ousegate, and was founded in 1859 by E. P. Brett, who converted a former oil cake mill and chemist's warehouse into a brewery. They traded as Brett Brothers from 1869. Brewing ceased on the acquisition by J Hunt, but the buildings were subsequently used by Hunt's as offices and stores, and still survive as Yates's.

Some Brett Brothers pubs: Achorne, St Martin's Lane, Cross Keys, Penley's Grove Street, Four Alls, Malton Road, Stockton on the Forest, Fox

The Half Moon Inn

Inn, Low Petergate, Golden Barrel, Walmgate, Malt Shovel, Walmgate, Robin Hood, Castlegate, Olde Starre Inn, Stonegate, Windmill, Blossom Street, Black Swan, Sutton on the Forest, Great Northern, Railway Street, Ouse Bridge Inn, King's Staithe, King William IV, Fetter Lane.

Hunt beers included a range of eight beers, including three milds, a bitter, Light Dinner Ale, Old Tom, India Pale Ale, and Double Brown Stout; to meet the increasing demand for its products, the Ebor Brewery was rebuilt in 1899. 1904 saw the purchase of the Tockwith brewery of Robert Brogden Sons & Co. Ltd, along with their 50 licensed houses, many of which were around Harrogate, Knaresborough and Northallerton.

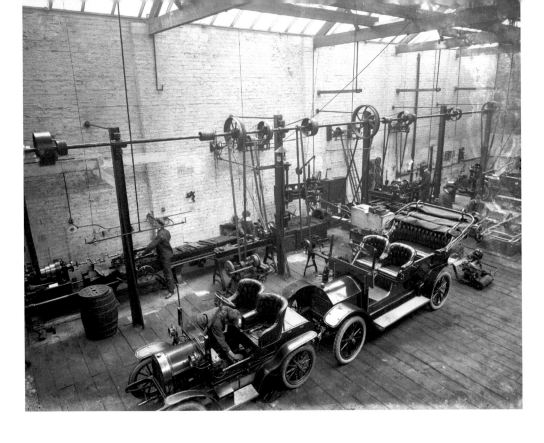

Gibbs Motor Manufacturers

Gibbs Motor Manufacturers and Russell's Motorbikes

The fascinating images here show Gibbs Motor Manufacturers in operation. John E. Gibbs and Co operated from premises in Thomas Street off James Street and seem to have specialised in steam cars and steam delivery vans.

C. S. Russell claimed to be York's largest motor cycle dealers – and we can see why. The business traded from two properties in the city: motor cycles were sold from this large depot on Lawrence Street.

The pedal cycles outlet was on the corner of Coppergate and Clifford Street. These premises are shown here when previously occupied by William Banks & Co., ham and cheese specialists.

York ham is a dry-cured ham; according to legend, it obtained its unique flavour from the sawdust from the oak timbers used in the building of York Minster. However, York hams have never been smoked although they are distinguished by the fact that the pigs' legs are long cut – they are rounded at the hip rather than squared off. *Law's Grocer's Manual* of 1949 tells us that 'In England the principal ham is long-cut, pale-dried dry-salt cured ham known as York Ham'. Other local delicacies include the popular York mayne bread; up until 1622 there were by-laws passed, urging people to bake it when spiced cake stole the market; this may have been in the form of Ouse

EASTER, 1937.   One day's output of
B.S.A. & NORTON MOTOR CYCLES LAWRENCE STREET DEPÔT
ESTABLISHED 1904

Bridge cakes known in the eighteenth century, a type of Yorkshire tea cake. There was also York Gingerbread, the recipe for which was included in Sarah Martin's 1795 *New Experienced English Housekeeper*, and Fulford Biscuits.

Ham, cheese and bicycles

Joseph Rowntree's

In 1890 Joseph Rowntree left the entirely unsuitable premises in Tanner's Moat and bought a twenty-nine-acre site to the north of York on Haxby Road. The objective: to build a highly efficient and ergonomic factory which would improve production techniques and transportation to meet the growing demand for their products in a pleasant working environment. In Joseph's own words he desired a workplace where his work force could 'develop all that is best and worthy in themselves'. Indeed 'healthful conditions of labour are not luxuries to be adopted or dispensed at will. They are conditions necessary for success.' Joseph was 'determined to spare neither pains nor money to incorporate the most complete and modern arrangements … for manufacturing purposes'.

Rowntree's, knocking off at Haxby Road

The Rowntree & Co. fire brigade

The company fire brigade comprised eighteen full-time staff; they had a fire engine, a steamer and an ambulance. During World War II the fire brigade comprised twenty-three full time and eighty part time staff, complemented by 145 fire guards. The air raid siren was on the top of the Elect Cocoa Block – throughout the war it sounded 140 times in blasts that lasted for 209 hours in total.

In World War II many companies, Mars for example, were either closed for the duration, transformed into completely different companies in support of the war effort (Rowntree's 'became' County Industries Ltd, or CIL, the secret Rowntree's company), or else they hosted other war manufacturers: Rowntree's, for example, manufactured Oxford Marmalade on behalf of Frank Cooper Ltd.

A prodigious amount of impromptu management and reorganisation went into converting Haxby Road into what was virtually a munitions factory housed in the Smarties Block. The definitive record of this fascinating chapter in the wartime lives of the staff, board and management at Rowntree's can be found in *The Cocoa Works in War-time* published by the company soon after the end of hostilities; here are some of the details recorded there: 13,000 square feet of floor space in the new office block was put at the disposal of 300 clerks of the Royal Army Pay Corps. The Fruit

Gum Department, at the request of the Ministry Of Food, manufactured jams and marmalade for Frank Cooper Ltd of Oxford. Part of the Almond Block extension was used by York firm Cooke, Troughton & Simms for the manufacture of military optical instruments. From the Cream Department came ersatz products such as National Milk Cocoa, Ryvita, Household Milk and Dried Egg.

The Card Box Mill replaced its production of fancy boxes to become a main supply depot for the RASC, Northern Command. The rest centre in the Dining Block was a refuge for blitzed families, mainly in the aftermath of the 1942 Baedeker raid after which it was requisitioned for five nights; a Voluntary Aid Detachment (VAD) hospital with 100 or so beds occupied the rest of the building. The nursery was also in there; this allowed mothers of children aged six months to five years of age to come to work. At any one time sixty children were looked after; cots and other furniture was made by the work's joiners and the orchard behind the Dining Block became the playground.

The target for CIL set by the Ministry Of Supply was 100,000 fuses per week, made mainly for shells used in twenty-five pounder guns; this was exceeded. By the end of the war CIL had also turned out four million anti-tank mine fuses. Workers in contact with explosive powder had to protect their skin and so 'make up' rooms were set up, where special face powder and topical creams were made available. Girls and women were advised to drink milk rather than tea or coffee at their mid-shift break. The sixty men and 850 women here worked alternate day and night shifts and were under the management of the aptly named Mr N. G. Sparkes; most of them had been transferred from production work in the Cocoa Works.

ARP work included the construction of three underground tunnel shelters in the orchard, rose garden and near the Wigginton Road entrance. The Estates Department was busy digging for victory: between 1939 and 1945 eight tons each of tomatoes, cabbage and onions, three tons of leeks and two tons of Brussel sprouts and 13,000 heads of lettuce along with smaller quantities of other vegetables were produced.

One of the most productive departments in the factory was the Chocolate Moulding Department which was engaged in the production of various types of war-time chocolate. Vitaminised plain chocolate was made for army rations and for distribution by UNRRA for the relief of starving children in Europe. Blended chocolate and vitaminised Plain York Chocolate was manufactured for prisoner-of-war parcels; at Christmas these were sent out with special wrappers.

Special chocolate 'Naps' in sealed tins were supplied to the Ministry of War Transport as emergency rations for use on ships, lifeboats and rafts. Pacific and Jungle Chocolate was specially produced to withstand high temperatures for troops and sailors in tropical climates. A similar type of 'unmeltable' chocolate is still produced in Australian chocolate factories today. Oatmeal Block and Fruit Bar was made for the servicemen in the Far East. US Army Field Ration Vitaminised chocolate, known as Ration D, was specially packed for the American forces. An Army Emergency Ration Special Chocolate that was hermetically sealed in tins was also manufactured along with special chocolate rations for air crew to eat after baling out.

The move to Haxby Road saw a growing headcount which coincided with a necessary change in factory discipline. Gone were the familiarity and personal contact between staff. Rules and regulations more appropriate to a large company were introduced from 1892. Time-keeping was formalised with doors opening at 6.00 am; staff not inside by 6.05 were excluded until 8.25 with the loss of a quarter of a day's pay. Two 'lates' in one week led to a week's suspension. Late-coming after breakfast and dinner were likewise not tolerated.

Rowntree's, Haxby Road

British Sugar Corporation, Poppleton

Building the British Sugar Corporation factory

This was built in 1926 by the Anglo-Scottish Beet Sugar Corporation with a slicing capacity of 1,000 tons a day. Rail was the method of choice for moving sugar beet until the development of road transport; consequently, much of the Poppleton site was originally given over to railway sidings. On arrival, wagons were driven over a weighbridge to assess gross weight and a sample was taken to calculate sugar content. Unloading then took place in the beet silo area, either by high pressure water jet (Elfa guns), by mechanical

Construction at the British Sugar Corporation factory

tipping or by pitchfork. Empty wagons were then reweighed to find the actual tonnage of beet delivered.

During the fourteen-week season the factory operated around the clock; 15–20,000 wagons passed through the factory in a season. A wagon was turned around every five or six minutes.

Harvesting the crop: back-breaking work picking the sugar beet for the British Sugar Corporation, Poppleton

York Station platforms

The platforms of the current York station built in the 1870s have been photographed many times. It appears Hanstock intended to produce a picture postcard from this view, adding his signature on the leg of the passenger bottom right of the card. The visible Enquiry Office sign indicates York Station served no fewer than four different railway companies at this time.

Platforms of the North Eastern Railway Station, York

York Waterworks

In 1908 York Waterworks Company issued a promotional brochure. The many photographs were the work of Thomas Hanstock.

External view of No 2 Engine House, erected in 1902. This was not used in the final brochure

Inside the engine house, York Waterworks Company

Standpipe on the inlet to the main raw water reservoir. This picture probably dates from 1902 when the height of the standpipe was increased

General view of the Acomb landing site positioned between the River Ouse and the East Coast Main Line

Clifton Scope and laying the water pipes

A second group of photographs relating to the York Waterworks Company shows the laying of a 15-inch diameter cast-iron water main under the river Ouse in 1904 at Clifton Scope. This main remains in use today immediately downstream of the 1960s Clifton Road Bridge.

Clifton Scope

Pipe-laying barges. Note the woman worker in the image below –
an unusual occupation for women in the early twentieth century

A professional diver with his state-of-the-art 1904 diving equipment and barges being used to lower the water main onto the river bed

Water pipes being laid

A river trip on the *River King* with Rowntree's factory
looming in the background

A busy River Ouse

The River Ouse has been crucial to York from earliest times, right through the Roman and Viking occupations and the Middle Ages, making York an important port. Evidence of Irish and German boats date from around 1125. The Romans called it Isis, the Saxons Youre and Eurewic. It often froze over in the early years of the twentieth century and skating on the river was very popular. The ice is said to have been up to twelve inches thick at times. Apart from skating, horse chestnut sellers set up braziers and stalls on the ice; there were even horse races between the Tower and Marygate in 1740 and football matches in 1607. In 1740 Thomas Gent set up his printing press on the ice, producing a leaflet to celebrate the event. The Ouse Navigation Trustees built the slipway at Clementhorpe in 1836 which gives its name to the pub there, The Slipway.

The Lowther Hotel is on the left in the image above, and Terry's can be seen in the distance on the right bank. Terry's moved to their purpose-built Baroque Revival building in 1930 from the Clementhorpe site which they had occupied since 1862. By 1840 Terry's products were being delivered to seventy-five towns all over England; products included candied eringo, coltfoot rock, gum balls and lozenges made from squill, camphor and horehound. Apart from boiled sweets they also made marmalade, marzipan, mushroom ketchup and calves' jelly. Conversation lozenges, precursors of Love Hearts (with such slogans as 'Can you polka?', 'I want a wife', 'Do you love me?' and 'How do you flirt?'), were particularly popular. Chocolate production began around 1867 with thirteen chocolate products adding to the other 380 or so confectionery and parfait lines. Before World War II 'Theatre Chocolates' were available with rustle-proof wrappers. The famous Chocolate Orange (which started life as a Chocolate Apple) was born in 1932 and at one point one in ten Christmas stockings reputedly contained a Terry's Chocolate Orange. In the 1990s seven million boxes of All Gold were sold in a year.

The Rowntree Railway

Rowntree Halt at Hambleton Terrace was a small, unmanned railway stop on the Foss Island's Branch Line on the southern edge of the chocolate factory. The LNER opened it in 1927 to provide an un-timetabled passenger service to the Rowntree factory for workers commuting from the Selby and

The Rowntree Halt

Doncaster areas. It was not much more than a signal and a single short platform situated a few yards west of the siding that allowed freight directly into the factory complex. There was no extra charge for the leg to the Halt from York station, either to the commuter or to Rowntree. The Halt was closed in 1988.

'Newton'

Between 1890 and 1895 Rowntree's bought one locomotive, *Marshall*, to assist in the construction of the Haxby Road factory, and had one-and-a-half miles of standard gauge track at their disposal. *Marshall* was sold in 1895 and *Newton* was then bought from T. A. Walker who had used it in the building of the Manchester Shipping Canal. It was put into use coal shunting at the factory. Locomotive No.2 was bought new in 1909 sharing general duties with a third locomotive bought in 1915. A fourth, the ramshackle *Swansea*, was bought in 1943 with its distinctive vivid green livery. The other locomotives were brown lined with cream. Rowntree also owned thirty-eight wagons. The company had seven miles of track and a short 18-inch narrow gauge line.

The line adjacent to the Rowntree factory

Derwent Valley Light Railway

DVLR was born of the Light Railways Act of 1896. Farmers south east of York needed a better way of reaching the markets at York and Selby with their produce than the existing rail routes could offer; a number of land owners approached Escrick and Riccall rural district councils to explore the possibility of a light railway. The result – DVLR – ran over sixteen miles from Layerthorpe to Cliff Common, a small station on the NER line between Selby and Market Weighton. The northern terminus at Layerthorpe linked into the NER's Foss Islands branch, and became DVLR headquarters. The ceremonial inaugural run of the Derwent Valley Light Railway took place on Saturday 21 July 1913 with the first operational journey on the following Monday.

Before boarding the ceremonial train, a blue silk ribbon was cut with specially made scissors by Lady Deramore, the wife of the Chairman of Directors.

The train left the Layerthorpe station in York, traveling 16 miles to Cliff Common before returning to York. The company directors were joined on the journey by a number of specially invited guests including the Lord Mayor and the Sheriff of York. Thomas Hanstock was also on board recording the

Lady Deramore cuts the ribbon before the ceremonial inaugural run of the Derwent Valley Light Railway

The DVLR at Elvington, with enthusiastic flag-waving crowds

The end of the line: the DVLR at Cliff Common

enthusiastic flag-waving crowds which greeted the train at all the interim stations at Osbaldwick, Murton Lane, Dunnington Halt, Dunnington, Elvington, Wheldrake, Cottingwith, Thorganby and Skipwith.

DVLR opened for goods and livestock in 1912 and for passengers in 1913 with three week-day trains in each direction and an extra service between Layerthorpe and Wheldrake. Scheduled time was fifty to fifty-eight minutes; carriages were first and third class, ex-NER painted dark blue with gold lettering. There were eleven stations on the line, from Layerthorpe south to Osbaldwick, Murton Lane, Dunnington Halt, Dunnington (for Kexby), Elvington, Wheldrake, Cottingwith, Thorganby, Skipwith and Cliff Common. All stations handled goods as well as passenger traffic and all had their own sidings. There was only ever one signal on the line, at Wheldrake, where a sharp bend immediately before the station hid the level crossing from the driver and demanded a warning. The original track was bought second hand from the Midland Railway's Settle–Carlisle line.

By 1916 passenger traffic from villages served along the Derwent was declining due to competition from bus services; in the 1920s passenger numbers dropped steeply from 49,000 at the end of World War I to 18,000 in 1925. Two Ford rail buses were introduced in 1924 coupled back to back but, despite reducing the cost to 5*d*. per mile from 1*s*., the line was closed for passenger traffic in 1926 although it was still used for healthy goods traffic until 1958.

From the 1930s goods traffic was on the up, expanding from the increasing Dig for Victory farm produce to include chemicals and minerals and benefitting from the restrictions on road transport caused by fuel rationing. During World War II the government built an aerodrome at Wheldrake, which became a supply dump for motor spirit; explosives and timber; mustard gas was stored at Cottingwith station. The line was never picked up by Luftwaffe reconnaissance because of the natural camouflage it obtained from weeds left to grow due to deferred maintenance.

The Derwent Valley Light Railway survived Grouping, and was never nationalised, and so has always been a private railway. The line is also known as the Blackberry Line – from the days when it was used to transport black-berries to markets in Yorkshire and London.

Most small towns and the larger villages had their own mills, now all long gone. Here are those at Wetherby, Boston Spa and Elvington.

The mill at Wetherby. The sign points us in the direction of
Harrogate Spa, some eight miles upstream
('FIRST TURN TO LEFT')

The mills at Boston Spa (above), and Elvington

Elvington was the base for Britain's only two Free French bomber squadrons (346 and 347): in 1945 a Halifax taking French aircrew home after the war crashed at Sheepwalk Farm, killing three Frenchmen. The last German plane to be shot down over Britain, a Junkers 88, crashed into a farm at Elvington in March 1945, killing two of the occupants. The dolphin fountain here was erected in 1897 to mark Victoria's diamond jubilee.

York's gasworks

In 1826 any town with a population exceeding 10,000 was likely to have had a gasworks. York was one of the first to get gas when, in 1824, the York Gas Light Company (YGLC) was established between the Foss and Monk Bridge and introduced York to gas lighting, or 'the lamp that wouldn't blow out'. The YGLC enjoyed a monopoly in gas supply until York Union Gas Light Company (YUGLC) set up their works in Hungate. After years of rivalry,

Construction of the gasometer

The new Klone Gasometer dominated the York skyline, standing just ten inches shorter than York Minster. What it lacked in height it also lacked in skyline aesthetics

with workmen from the former surreptitiously filling in the latter's excavations, they merged in 1847 to form the York United Gas Light Company, later shortened to the York Gas Company, operating at both the Hungate and Monk Bridge sites, but in 1850 the Hungate works were closed. Due to restrictions on space at the Old Works at Monk Bridge, a completely new works was built at Heworth Green in 1885 – the New Works.

Before the railways came coal was shipped to the gas works from the York & North Midland Railway staiths on the Ouse, then along the Foss – or through the congested city on carts. As soon as the new site was mooted a rail junction connecting to the NER Foss Islands Branch was constructed allowing for the easier movement of 50,000 tons of coal. The railway opened in 1915 and was in service until 1959 with locomotives operating on an electrified railway – names were *Kenneth* built in 1885 arriving in 1919, and *Centenary* built in 1924; livery was olive green with red, yellow and gold lettering. The power supply came from a direct current of 500 volts along a private line from the Corporation Power Station.

The effect of chimney smoke on the city, 1931

The pair of photographs on the opposite page shows the effects of chimney smoke in the city. A note found in one box of original glass negatives written by Thomas Hanstock's son Peter details who commissioned the photographs and why. The note reads 'These plates were taken by T J W Hanstock for the York Health Authority to illustrate the effect of chimney smoke over the city of York. Some of the views were taken on Sundays (min smoke) and others on weekdays. The photos were taken from the top of the Klone Gasometer (200ft high) during 1931'.

Rowntree's and Quakerism

There is an inextricable association between English chocolate manufacturing with the Society of Friends, or Quakerism. Fry, Cadbury, Rowntree and Thorne of Leeds were all Quakers. Why was it that the chocolate industry at the end of the nineteenth century and in the early years of the twentieth prospered largely under Quaker ownership? It is all the more remarkable, though, when we remember that in 1851 Quakers accounted for less than 0.1 per cent of the 21 million population of England. 'Friends' were excluded from the only teaching universities in England at the time, Oxford and Cambridge, because of their non-conformism and the universities' association with Anglicanism; they were debarred from Parliament and the guilds; they were restricted in what they could and could not do as lawyers because they refused to take oaths; the arts were considered frivolous and they were disqualified from the armed services because they were usually pacifists.

One of the few alternatives left to well-to-do young Quakers was to pursue a life in industry or business, and this is what many did. In doing so they often brought with them a tradition of high quality management and fair trading practices, rigorous scientific research and innovative technical development, as well as a preoccupation with quality and a breathtakingly detailed attention to commercial administration. So Quakers entered business and industry: one of the emerging industries at the time was cocoa and chocolate – this was partly a result of increased affordability amongst the working classes who had more disposable income, lower taxes on imports which reduced prices in the shops, and improvements in quality, a better taste and less adulteration. What had been a luxury for the few was fast becoming an affordable indulgence for many. Moreover, cocoa and chocolate chimed perfectly with Quaker views on temperance; they were healthy beverages too, because their consumption entailed boiling what was often unclean water. One of the legacies of the frequent Meetings routinely held by Quakers

Transporting cocoa to the Rowntree's factory

to spread the word was the building up of a strong network of dependable friends and contacts; this in turn, along with intermarriage amongst Quaker families, led to a tradition of mutual assistance and an ethical, enlightened attitude in business and industry, and to strong industrial partnerships, underpinned by unfaltering service and philanthropy to the community at large. All of this manifested itself in York at Rowntree's; as such Quakerism has had an immeasurable effect on the city in every way – commercially, socially, educationally and physically – for over a century.

Electricity in York

The lights first went on in York in 1899. The ground around the station (run by York Corporation Electricity Committee) vibrated with the noise and the 30,000 horse power created by the generating station. Today, the chimney has survived but all else is gone.

Nichols Electricity

Leetham's flour mill

The banks of the River Foss were one of the least picturesque parts of York. Dating originally from the 1890s, the giant Leetham's flour mill straddled both banks of the river at Hungate. This was one of the largest flour mills in Europe, designed by Walter Penty in 1895, comprising five storeys and a nine-storey water tower complete with battlements and turrets. It is surrounded on three sides by the Foss and Wormald's Cut. By 1911 more than 600 people worked here.

Leetham & Sons were one of the biggest firms not just in York but in the British flour-milling industry in the second half of the nineteenth century. The Hungate flour mill was founded by Henry Leetham in 1860 and extended to the Foss site in 1885. After Castle Mills lock was rebuilt in 1888, Leetham's was one of the chief users of the river, with access by a four-storey high level gantry bridge across the Foss to Hungate Mills. By 1900 Leetham's had expanded with operations in Hull, Newcastle and Cardiff. Leetham's in York was producing 112 sacks per hour by this time.

Initially, around 1900, railway activity was confined to the warehouse on the Foss Islands side of the River Ouse where four horses were used for shunting as NER locomotives were prohibited from crossing Foss Islands Road. In 1904 Leetham's was denied permission to deploy steam engines to haul wheat wagons from their sidings due to the un-navigability of the Ouse. In 1919 it seems that this decision was finally reversed and steam haulage began.

Leethams flour mill on Foss Bank

Leetham ran three locomotives: *Neptune* (1863), *Tissington* (1893) and one other – although never at the same time. Essentially, bulk grain arrived at the mill in barges and bagged flour and meal left by train after overnight loading. The daily total was twelve to twenty wagons although up to 100 was not unknown. The famous steam paddle tub *Anglia* was owned by Leetham's; this was the vessel which had towed Cleopatra's needle from Egypt to England and had come to York in 1916 to be converted into a store ship.

Spillers took Leetham's over in 1930 before removing to Hull in 1931 after a fire; Rowntree's bought it in 1937 for cocoa bean storage.

Biology at Bootham School

✌ Schools ✌

WILLIAM TUKE (1732–1822) FIRST RAISED THE idea in 1818 of setting up a boys' school in York for the sons of Quakers 'and any children of the opulent who will submit themselves to the general system of diet and discipline'. In 1822 premises on Lawrence Street were leased from the Retreat, and the school opened in early 1823 as the York Friends Boys' School, or 'The Appendage'. In 1829 it had become known as Yorkshire Quarterly Meeting Boys' School – its official name until 1889 – even after it had moved to 20 (now 51) Bootham in 1846.

It was the school's proximity to the River Foss that triggered the move to more salubrious premises. One master even carried a pistol to shoot the rats, while cholera was also a problem. In the late nineteenth century many of the Rowntree family boys were educated at Bootham; one of them, Arthur Rowntree (or Chocolate Jumbo to give him his nickname), was Headmaster (1899–1927). The school had a tradition of taking disadvantaged boys from the Lawrence Street area on a Lads' Camp, usually at Robin Hood's Bay, and this endured well into the twentieth century. Arthur Rowntree said: 'We are proud to be in the tradition of promoting friendship between all classes'. A number of staff and scholars were influential in the political and social reforms of their times, not least Seebohm Rowntree (Bootham 1882–87).

Bootham Natural History Society was established in 1834 by John Ford, superintendent or head from 1829 to 1865. Its full name was 'The Natural History, Literary and Polytechnic Society' and as such was the umbrella organisation for many other clubs. The school was moved to Roman Catholic Ampleforth during World War II; Donald Gray, the head at the time, is reputed to have addressed the combined school as 'Friends, Romans and Countrymen'.

Bootham was not the only boys' Quaker School in York: in 1827 the Hope Street British School was established and attended by many children of Friends; it was slightly unusual because, in addition to the usual curriculum, it taught the working of the Electric Telegraph with the Electric Telegraph Company supplying the instruments, and the school reciprocating by supplying the company with clerks.

Bootham School biology, above, and natural history, below

Woodwork classes at Bootham School

Metalwork, Bootham School

And so to bed …

The church-like John Bright Library

In 1899 almost the entire school was destroyed by fire: a keen pupil was boiling snail shells in the Natural History room when he was summoned by the bell for reading, and the snails were left boiling all night … on being informed by the fire brigade that his school was a smouldering shell the headmaster fell on his sword and promptly resigned. The accidental arsonist later became a farmer but sadly his bad luck prevailed when he blew himself up while uprooting a tree.

The Mount School

The story of The Mount School begins with Esther Tuke, second wife of William Tuke, who in 1785 opened the boarding school in Trinity Lane, off Micklegate and known then as the Friends' Girls' School. The aims of the York school were heavily influenced by the famous Quaker school at Ackworth near Pontefract, founded in 1779 by John Fothergill and which, in turn, was previously a (particularly insalubrious) branch of the London Foundling Hospital in Bloomsbury. Fothergill, a Quaker physician, teamed up with William Tuke and David Barclay (of banking fame) to open the school for Quaker children 'not of affluence'; despite best intentions it had a

A lesson at the Mount School

The Mount School: physical training

reputation for being 'harsh, if not barbarous'. Pupils included the daughters of Abraham Darby III of Coalbrookdale, the famous ironmaker. In 1796 purpose-built premises were bought for £450 in Tower Street near to York Castle and the Friends' Meeting House. William Tuke retired in 1804 with the school in financial difficulties; it closed in 1812.

In 1829 Samuel Tuke established the York Friends' Boys' School (later Bootham School) and then turned his attentions to establishing a girls' equivalent along the same lines. This materialised in Castlegate House in 1831, the 1763 mansion of the Recorder of York. Girls attended the lectures given by the Yorkshire Philosophical Society, adding to and annotating their own collections of shells, minerals and pressed plants. In 1855 the lease on Castlegate expired, thus triggering the move to the purpose-built buildings at the Mount under the supervision of Rachel Tregelles. Lydia Rous took over as superintendent in 1866 and it was she who ensured that Mount girls entered the new public examinations. The University of London was not interested; to them 'girls were poorly educated and therefore incapable of taking a degree course' but Cambridge University, which established Emily Davies' Girton College for women in 1873, took them on board. Alumni include actors Mary

Ure and Dame Judi Dench, the three Drabble sisters (writers A. S. Byatt and Margaret, and art historian Helen Langdon); astronomer Jocelyn Bell Burnell; and TV correspondent Kathy Killick.

Interior and exterior views of the Mount School

The school moved to its present site on the Mount in 1856. Hanstock photographed the girls engaged in private study and exercising in the old gymnasium, which was transformed into the Art Wing following the opening of a new gymnasium and swimming pool in the 1960s. Also shown is the new Assembly Hall built in contemporary style around 1930.

In 1901, under the aegis of Winifred Sturge, a graduate of London University's Westfield College, the Mount Junior School opened, founded on Montessori principles and included amongst its former pupils the Marxist historian Christopher Hill, six of the children of Arnold and Mary Rowntree and William Sessions, the York printer and publisher, and his sister.

Haxby Road School

Haxby Road School was opened by the Lord Mayor of York, Alderman R. H. Vernon Wragge in January 1904. The school was designed by leading York architect W. H. Brierley. It was one of the first of its kind to incorporate a large central hall to maximise light and air in the classrooms.

It also featured a hot water system, ample tarmacked playgrounds and play sheds for wet weather. The school was built to accommodate 1,200 pupils at a cost of just under £20,000.

External view of Haxby Road School

Inside the hall at Haxby Road School

Archbishop Holgate Grammar School

The school is, after St Peter's, the oldest in York, and was founded as Archbishop Holgate's Grammar School in 1546 by Robert Holgate, financed by capital from the Dissolution of the Monasteries. The original grammar school was in Ogleforth and known as The Reverend Shackley's School; Thomas Cooke taught here, the famous optical instrument manufacturer who went on to establish T. Cooke & Sons, later Cooke, Troughton & Simms, the equally famous telescope manufacturers. In 1858 the school merged with the Yeoman School when it moved to Lord Mayor's Walk; it relocated again in 1963 to its present site in Badger Hill.

Chemistry teachers and old boys Albert Holderness and John Lambert are the authors of one of the most successful school chemistry books ever published: *School Certificate Chemistry*, published in 1936. The 500,000th copy came off the press in 1962.

Archbishop Holgate was the first protestant archbishop, in 1545, and the first to marry. He deserted both his religion and his wife when the Catholic Mary Tudor acceded to the throne in 1553.

A portrait of Mr P. J. Vinter, Headmaster of Archbishop Holgate
Grammar School (1915–37), and his family

This picture shows Mr Vinter's son proudly displaying what appear to be 'Meccano' constructions. 'Meccano' is a model construction system created in 1898 by Frank Hornby in Liverpool

Pupils from the school giving a gymnastic display. These images were taken outside the school and headmaster's house. This must have been a welcome commission for Hanstock as the school, situated in Lord Mayor's Walk, was situated less than 300 yards from his premises at 11 Clarence Street

Earlier in 1909, Hanstock had photographed the school's old boys'
cricket match. The playing field on Wigginton Road was also close
to Hanstock's premises

St John Ambulance outside the Minster

⁓ Hospitals ⁓

S T John Ambulance is the collective name of a number of affiliated organisations largely run by volunteers around the world. It runs courses and provides first aid and emergency medical services. These organisations are overseen by the international Order of St John.

One marvelous production which rolled out of York Carriage Works during World War I was the ambulance train made from existing carriage rolling stock; it comprised sixteen carriages and was known as 'Continental Ambulance Train Number 37'. It was 890 feet 8 inches long and weighed 465 tons when loaded, without a locomotive. Painted khaki it bore the Geneva Red Cross painted on the window panels and frames on each of the carriages on both sides.

VAD (Voluntary Aid Detachment) hospitals were one of many ways in which York made ready for total war. Castle Yard became an internment

The VAD Hospital at York St John

camp for aliens with room for 40,000, apparently, as did a field hospital in Leeman Road. The Cattle Market became a horse depot. The military requisitioned the De Grey Rooms, the Exhibition Hall and the Railway Institute; Knavesmire was a drill ground; an aerodrome was built at Copmanthorpe; 700 Belgian refugees were lodged in private houses in New Earswick and York; a canteen for travelling troops opened on York railway station; VAD hospitals opened in Clifford Street and at St John's College; stranded soldiers were given supper, bed and breakfast in the Assembly Rooms – 435 in one record night with over 100,000 all told. A munitions factory was opened in Queen Street in two sheds hired from NER employing 1,000, mainly women and girls. By the second week of the war registered aliens filled the Castle Prison with more held in a property in Leeman Road. Just before 1914, there were already 1,600 men in the army from a labour force of 35,000.

The VAD was a voluntary force made up of civilians deployed to providing nursing care for wounded military personnel in the United Kingdom and in various other countries in the British Empire. VADs were never military nurses as such and were not under military control, even though they were

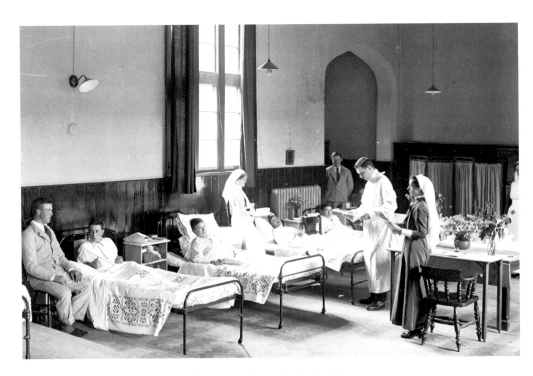

Ward rounds at York St John

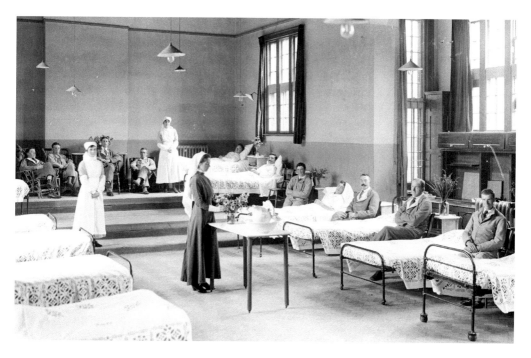

On the ward at York St John

inextricably connected with and major contributors to the national war effort. Military nursing was under the auspices of the Queen Alexandra's Royal Army Nursing Corps, the Princess Mary's Royal Air Force Nursing Service, and the Queen Alexandra's Royal Naval Nursing Service. VAD nurses worked in field hospitals and in places of recuperation in the UK.

The VADs were founded in 1909 with the collaboration of the British Red Cross and Order of St John. By 1914 there were over 2,500 Voluntary Aid Detachments in Britain. Of the 74,000 VAD members in 1914, two-thirds were women and girls. Two years later the military hospitals in the UK were staffed by 8,000 trained nurses with about 126,000 beds; overseas in various locations there were 4,000 nurses with 93,000 beds. By 1918 the total number of VADs was about 80,000: 12,000 nurses working in the military hospitals and 60,000 unpaid volunteers working in auxiliary hospitals of one sort or another.

VAD hospitals in York other than York St John included Nunthorpe Hall. Sir Edward Lycett Green gave his extensive house for use by the VAD; he carried all expenses not covered by the government grant. The hospital was run by his daughter-in-law as Commandant. The Hall was demolished

Preparing a hospital meal at York St John

in 1977; the site is built over as Coggan Close, between Albemarle Road and Philadelphia Terrace. The hospital opened its wards on 1 October 1915, with a convoy of men direct from the Battle of Loos. It started with 50 beds in eight wards rising to 76 beds. On its closure on 14 April 1919, 915 patients had been treated.

The night of 2/3 May 1916 saw the hospital bombed in a Zeppelin raid, setting fire to the house and forcing the hospital to be evacuated. Trained staff included one matron and three sisters; matron and two sisters lived in. There were 24 VADs, including two cooks and two charwomen. The Medical Officers were Dr Louise Fraser and Dr Armytage.

Dr Fraser's medical career in York started at the York Dispensary, providing free home care for the poor of the city. In 1906 she set up her own practice while continuing to work at the Dispensary; she also held a weekly clinic for women and children which ultimately led to the establishment of the first maternity home in York in Ogleforth with five beds. From this was born the Infant Welfare Scheme, responsible for improving the nutrition of new mothers. Dr Fraser was Medical Officer at Clifford Street Hospital from May to December 1915, and Medical Officer at Nunthorpe Hall from 18 July until February 1918. During her time at Nunthorpe Hall Dr Fraser was paid the sum of 3*d*. per bed. (I am grateful to Clements Hall Local History Group's

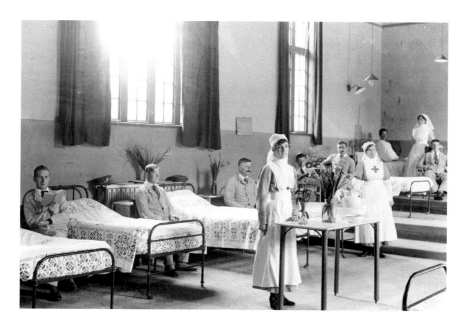

Bootham School VAD hospital

'Nunthorpe Hall: The Story of an Auxiliary Hospital in World War One', from which the above is paraphrased; http://www.clementshallhistorygroup.org.uk/projects/world-war-1/the-contribution-of-women-in-the-first-warl/nunthorpe-hall-the-story-of-an-auxiliary.)

Clifford Street was another VAD Hospital, in the Friends' Meeting House in Friargate. The hospital was opened on 23 March 1915 with 40 beds which later increased to 56. It closed on 10 January 1919, having treated 819 patients.

Bootham School VAD hospital was established in 1914, allegedly on the strength of rumours of impending naval battles in the North Sea. Bootham School was converted into a 100-bed hospital in 17 days but the battles failed to materialise and, after six weeks, it was stood down and converted back to a school. Term started eleven days late. After the war, it became known that there had been bombardments of Hartlepool, Whitby and Scarborough by cruisers of the German fleet, but whether anyone in York heard of the bombings at the time is questionable.

York St John's roots go back to 1841 when the York Diocesan Training School, for teacher education, opened in May 1841 with one pupil on the register, sixteen-year-old Edward Preston Cordukes. The Students' Union building is today named after him. The school was founded by the Church of England and teacher training here focused on church schools. The relationship of education and religion is still part of the fabric. The college changed its name to St John's College in the late 1890s. By 1904 St John's was the largest Diocesan College in the country with 112 students. In 1916, half way through the Great War, the college was forced to close because all the male students had left for the front. The building was requisitioned as a VAD hospital until it re-opened in 1919. The affiliated women's college in Ripon remained operational, however, and these students were able to make clothes, bandages and splints for the soldiers. Ripon and York merged to become the College of Ripon & York St John in 1974. By 2001 all taught courses moved to the York campus and the name York St John was adopted.

Other medical facilities in York were pressed into war service; this report from the *Yorkshire Herald* sums up the situation:

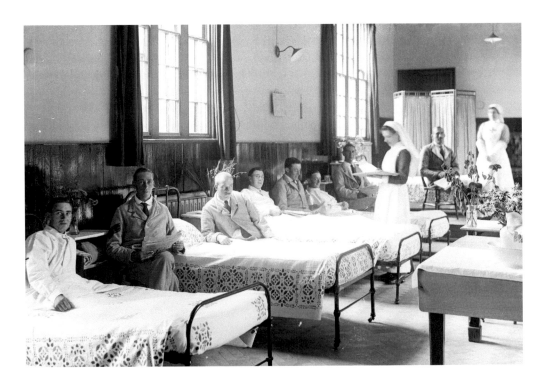

York St John

Patients and staff at York St John

On Friday September 6th, 1918, a convoy of 160 wounded soldiers arrived by train into York City Station at 3.30am. They were met by members of the newly formed Women's Department of Stretcher Bearers, who, under the supervision of Colonel F. W. Lamballe, assisted in the transport of 30 men to York County Hospital. A further 50 men were sent to the Central Military Hospital on Fulford Road, which extended its buildings to meet this additional demand. The largest group of 80 soldiers was transferred to the Haxby Road Military Hospital (Rowntree's dining block).

Psychological illnesses were a major problem, often undiagnosed or mis-diagnosed. Nevertheless, treatment was available at Naburn Hospital (then York City Asylum), Clifton Hospital, Bootham Hospital and The Retreat, all of which cared for patients diagnosed with 'shell-shock', many of whom remained as patients long after the war had ended.

Nursing staff of the York County Hospital. This and the following
three photographs were taken between 1928 and 1929.
Here, in the grounds of the nurses' home with the city walls as a
backdrop, are some of the meticulously turned out
senior nursing staff in 1928

York County Hospital

York County Hospital opened in a rented house in 1740 in Monkgate.
Before that, from 1614, the City Surgeon was responsible for medical care. In
1745 a purpose-built hospital opened on the same site with fifty beds: 2,417
patients had been treated by 1750. As a charitable hospital (where the finan-
ciers could choose who received treatment there) the County Hospital was
not responsible for the city's sick poor; this led to the establishment of the
Dispensary. The 1745 hospital building was demolished in 1851 and replaced
with a new 100-bed hospital costing £11,000. In 1887 it merged with the
York Eye Institution which had opened in 1875.

The present 600-bed York District Hospital opened in 1976, replacing the County Hospital, Fulford Hospital, Deighton Grove Hospital, Yearsley Bridge Hospital, Acomb Hospital, the Military Hospital and City Hospital. The eighteenth century also saw the founding of York Lunatic Asylum and the revolutionary Retreat for the humane care of the mentally ill.

Christmas on the children's ward, Victoria Ward, 1928

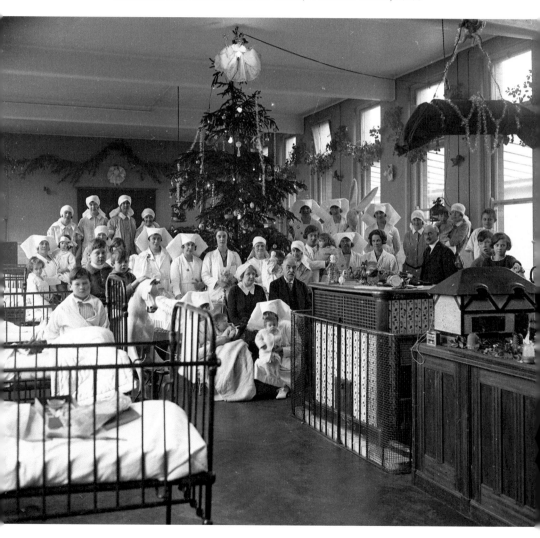

Thomas Hanstock was a regular visitor to York District Hospital situated less than a mile from his home and business premises. He regularly assisted by taking X-rays and the more usual type of photographs of the buildings, wards, patients and staff.

Easily the saddest picture in the book. Infants on the Balkan Frame ward. The Balkan frame is a frame employed in the treatment of fractured bones of the leg or arm that provides overhead weights and pulleys for suspension, traction, and continuous extension of the splinted fractured limb.
This particular photograph was used as publicity to raise funds for orphans and for the treatment of disadvantaged children

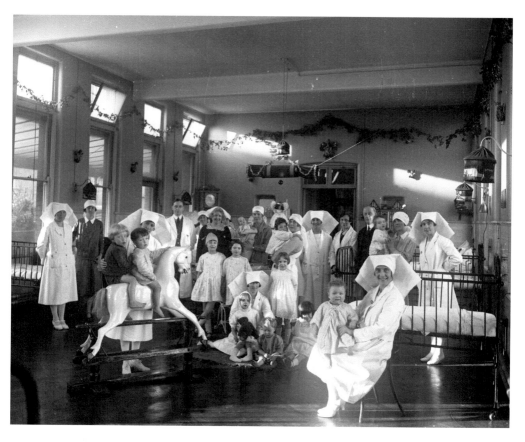

Christmas on the children's ward, Victoria Ward, 1928

York Co-op

❧ Shops ❧

I N 1909 THE YORK EQUITABLE INDUSTRIAL Society Ltd published a 'Jubilee History' to mark its fiftieth year. Thomas Hanstock was commissioned to photograph the Society's properties to illustrate the book. Shown here are the Central York premises, 20–30 Railway Street.

The Co-op in Willis Street

The Cemetery Road butcher's, with slaughter house behind

A Co-op exhibition display

York Co-op at a trade exhibition

York Co-op warehouse: the coal depot, bakery and bacon factory
on the bank of the river Ouse at Clementhorpe

Dove & Son's ironmongers in Pavement, with workshops
in Lady Peckitt's Yard

Inside Dove & Sons, hardware and gardening

Inside Dove & Sons, domestic appliances

In 1939 William Dove died aged 84; he was managing director of W. Dove & Sons Limited ironmongers and ironfounders, a business founded by his grandfather in 1804.

W. Bellerby & Sons, at 85 Micklegate. 'Sign writers, house and church' presumably meant their skills were suitable for all kinds of establishment. Other interesting businesses on Micklegate were the Danish Pure Butter Company at number 33 (the famous Butter Market used to be here), and the Midland Artificial Teeth Association at 14, makers of artificial teeth, unsurprisingly!

J. B. Inglis & Sons

Established in 1885, the J. B. Inglis & Sons showrooms were at 4 Coney Street (originally in Clifford Street) while the Crown Plating works were in Castlegate. Harness, carriage, motor-car and bicycle fittings were a specialty and their Kohinoor silver and plate polish provided the 'perfect polish' in liquid and powder form.

Instead of waiting for the Corporation to supply his electricity, Mr Inglis 'put down a small installation to light his premises' in the 1880s. His Sheffield suppliers of silver offered 5,000 lines 'all of which are practically in stock, as a wire will bring down any article by the first train'. The showroom for clocks was behind the shop 'where a wedding ring may be fitted without fear of interruption from other customers'.

Pearce & Sons – Diamond Merchants – were next to the post office in Lendal. Edward Jackson in Coney Street specialised in pearls and 'a fashionable assortment of Mourning Rings', while near neighbours Robert Cattle and James Barber were famous for their silver tokens, which were issued and redeemable at their face value in lieu of cash.

Halford's Cycle Company

Halfords was not at Foss Islands Road as it is today, but 26 Market Street, next door to Burton's the butchers and below the Refuge Insurance Company. Tomlinson's were next door the other way, suppliers of Spratt's dog cakes and puppy biscuits, while Clues Brothers, seedsmen and florists, were at 23.

Here is a brief early history of Halford's:

> 1892: Halfords Cycle Company Limited was formed by Mr F. W. Rushbrooke in Birmingham, England, as a local hardware store. In 1902, Rushbrooke moved to a store on Halford Street in Leicester, after which the company was named, and started selling cycling goods.

> 1910: A further 110 retail stores were opened to the public throughout England.

> 1931: The 200th store opened.

1934: The first Scottish store opened in Glasgow.

1939–40: With many members of the workforce serving their country at war, wives and families of managers took over running the stores.

1945: Bought the Birmingham Bicycle Company.

1955: The main Corporation Street building in Birmingham burned to the ground, although just 10 days later the company was back up and running in a temporary building in Kyotts Lake Road.

1957: Halfords celebrated its 50th Jubilee year.

Pianoforte dealers Noyes with their teaching and practising rooms were at 12 Tower Street, hemmed in by dressmakers: Booker, Miss G. at number 11, and Chaloner, Miss M. at number 14.

J. Noyes & Son, the piano people

Sampson's Library and Bookshop

At 13 Coney Street, next to Leak & Thorpe. York has an impressive tradition of publishing, printing and bookselling and was for many years only bettered by London, Oxford and Cambridge. William Alexander was one of York's earliest booksellers and printers; trading from Castlegate he refused to publish novels, considering them far too ephemeral. His self-censorship was to cost him dearly, if this story is to be believed. Walter Scott, while researching *Ivanhoe*, came to York and visited Alexander's bookshop where he suggested Alexander might publish his book. Alexander declined, saying 'I esteem your friendship but I fear thy books are too worldly for me to print'. He paid for his rebuff, though, as the bookseller is thought to be the boring Dr Dryasdust to whom Scott dedicated *Ivanhoe*.

In 1796 Alexander married Ann Tuke, daughter of William Tuke. Ann Alexander was the author of a pamphlet campaigning against the exploitation of children and specifically against the employment of climbing boys in 1817. Castlegate is the setting for Walter Scott's the Seven Stars where Jeanie Deans stayed en route to London in *Heart of Midlothian*.

Arthur Andersons (Sotheran's) Booksellers was also in Coney Street in 1837, the latest in a long line of York booksellers stretching back to Francis Hildyard's shop established 'at the sign of The Bible, Stonegate' in 1682. In 1763 this became John Todd and Henry Sotheran until 1774 when

Sotheran set up on his own next to St Helen's church, soon moving across the Square to where the Savings Bank was. Henry Cave's late eighteenth-century Todd's Book and Print Warehouse, as with many booksellers of the time, was something of an apothecary's store too, with a popular line in rat poison, negus and lemonade and similar preparations and confections. Roman busts watched over the 30,000 or so books. The Book Saloon at 6 Micklegate stocked 'the largest and best selection in the North of England', according to *York in 1837*, which goes on to tell us that the bookshop 'meets the demand for healthy literature engendered by the rapid growth of education and educational facilities'. Thomas Wilson at the Dryden's Head – Bookseller, Stationer, Printer Etc sold fancy goods, local guidebooks and postcards in Coney Street, before that in High Ousegate and Pavement, and Cash Stationery Store in Bridge Street offered 'a wide range of funeral cards'. John Wolstenholme sold books in Minster Gates, his building graced by his brother's fine statue of Minerva. Other evidence for this bookish aspect of York society is the red Printer's Devil at Coffee Yard, off Stonegate. Today, independent bookselling survives with the Little Apple near the Minster.

F. R. Delittle were Fine Art Printers at the Eboracum Letter Factory, 6 Railway Street, later moving to Vine Street. Founded in 1888 they were publishers of the *Yorkshire Chronicle and Delittle's York Advertiser* which had a circulation of 12,000 copies in 1897. They also produced the *City Chronicle and Sheffield Advertiser;* staff numbered sixty in 1900. Books published included *Eboracum, The Yorkshire Road Book* and *Delittle's Picturesque York* as well as *York in 1837*. They were particularly noted for the world famous top quality wooden type used for railway posters, theatre bill boards and shop window advertisements. Delittle closed in 1997 but their fame lives on in the Type Museum in London which displays a reconstruction of the Delittle type room.

Thomas Godfrey was a phrenologist who invented his qualifications; he opened his first bookshop at 46½ Stonegate in 1895 selling second hand books 'recently purchased from private libraries'. The business was called 'Ye Olde Boke Shoppe' but it failed: Godfrey 'became dissatisfied of the apathy of the citizens and disposed of the business' – sentiments and actions which could be echoed by many an independent bookseller today. An alternative report, though, attributes his failure to the selling of Oscar Wilde's *Portrait of Dorian Gray* after it had been recalled by the publishers, thus giving 'offence to some of the good people in York by his handling of a book which was regarded at the time as a most indecent publication'. Godfrey tried again in 1904 at 37 Goodramgate with the Eclectic Book Company, eventually moving back to 16 Stonegate with a business imaginatively named The Book Company, later Edward S. Pickard. In 1982 the business moved over the road to 32 Stonegate and acquired a second shop on the campus at York University which now trades as Blackwells.

The Leak & Thorp fire

In 1933, a fire broke out which totally destroyed the Leak & Thorp shop, although it was up and running again within a year. The chocolate must have been melting in the Black Boy Chocolate shop next door! In the mid-1920s Rowntree's bought Fuller & Maynard's Black Boy shops.

The Coney Street department store offered – as do department stores today – a wide range of clothing, carpets and furniture. An interesting line was their portmanteaux, dress baskets, suit cases and luncheon baskets. Leak & Thorp was often referred to as the 'Selfridges of York'; it opened its doors on 11 March 1848, when William Leak set up at 35 Parliament Street, soon to be joined in business by Mr H. B. Thorp. In 1869, the shop moved to Coney Street, on the site of late lamented George Hotel.

The fire at the Leak and Thorp department store

Boyes fire and collapse

The devastating fire at the Boyes building on Ouse Bridge, 8 November 1910, started on the second of six floors when paper decorations in the toy department were set alight by a nearby gas lamp. Despite the best efforts of the fire brigade, assisted by the Rowntree Fire Brigade, the building was a smouldering shell six hours later. Boyes' Scarborough store also burnt down, in 1914. The old York shop had been trading since 1906; Boyes' new shop was completed in July 1912 and closed down in 1983, to reopen in Goodramgate in 1987. Hundreds watched the fire fighters tackle the blaze from Ouse Bridge.

The reconstruction included a 10-foot red brick clock tower on top of a 60-foot reinforced concrete building. In February 1912 the partly built clock tower collapsed, crashing through three floors to the basement. One of the many men working on the site was killed, two others were seriously injured requiring hospital treatment, and a number of others sustained minor injuries. Before the accident the lower floors were opened by Boyes & Company, to catch the 1911 Christmas trade. The new store finally opened in July 1912. The building ceased to be a Boyes store in February 1983.

The collapsed Boyes building

Testing the load-bearing strength of the new building after the
collapse of the tower

The collapsed
floor inside the
Boyes building

Cussins & Light

The light first went on for Cussins & Light in 1919 when Pat Light and Regge Cussins met on 4 January 1919 at the 13th Group Headquarters of the RAF based at Chester. Two years later Regge opened a workshop in St Andrewgate hoping to do business as a 'woodworker, electrical and general engineer'. Pat joined him a few weeks later after his discharge from the RAF. Speaking in 1961, Regge takes up the story:

> Our first radio set was a three-valve model using bright-emitter valves which consumed the full charge of a six-volt car battery in 15 hours. I shall always remember the first time we got it to work. It was about 9.30 one evening in the autumn of 1922 and we tuned into London Station 2LO and the Savoy Orpheans. We had three pairs of headphones and we split them into single ear-pieces and grabbed everyone we could find to come and listen. We have seen many wonderful developments in electronics since then, but none of them have ever given us quite such a thrill.

Cussins and Light at a radio show in the Assembly Rooms

Their first retail premises were at 34 Walmgate, initially in 1925 allocating equal space to motorbikes and 'wireless'. However within two years the motorbikes had gone and 'wireless' in component, kit and fully built-up form had taken over completely.

The job which really established Cussins & Light was the installation of electric lighting powered by a generator with battery accumulator back-up at Sutton Hall, Sutton-on-the-Forest. Because electrification did not reach rural areas until the '50s, if you wanted electric lighting in your country house in the 1920s you had to have your own generating plant.

Number 1, King's Square opened for business in June 1934 and with it the exclusive Murphy dealership for York. Regge was issued with the first television licence issued in the York area on 8 March 1948. It cost £2 and enabled him to watch the grainy pictures from the Alexandra Palace, London transmitter. He erected a 60ft aerial on his bungalow in Garrow Hill and used a Murphy V114 – the 9" television set for the pictures.

1986 saw the beginning of the process to convert Cussins & Light into a property company and two years later they transformed a fire gutted woollen warehouse in Melrose Yard, Walmgate, York into a three-storey office block. In 2008 they bought their first overseas properties, in Berlin and in 2012 three properties in Leipzig were purchased.

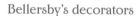

Bellersby's decorators

Boroughbridge

◦◦ Villages & small towns ◦◦

Thomas Hanstock published postcards from the photographs he took of many of the small towns and country villages close to York. In his day, venturing even a few miles out of the city was not without its challenges, not least the need to carry his cumbersome photographic equipment. Here are some of his views of villages, many characterised still with their dirt roads. It is probable that the villagers he encountered had never seen a camera, or even travelled as far as York.

Boroughbridge

The Romans built a fort near the Devil's Arrows to defend a crossing of the River Ure. The Normans moved this wooden bridge to its present site in the late eleventh century; it was eventually rebuilt in stone in the sixteenth century. A plaque tells us that the downstream side dates from 1562 and the upstream from 1784 after it had been widened. In 1318 and 1319 the town was devastated by marauding Scots and at the 1322 Battle of Boroughbridge Sir Andrew Harclay defeated the Earl of Lancaster who took refuge in the old church on St James's Square; notwithstanding, Harclay took Lancaster prisoner and had him tried and beheaded as a traitor at York. Harclay was elevated to Earl of Carlisle but turned against Edward and was himself beheaded in 1323. His name lives on in the Harclay Bar in Rose Manor Hotel. The Crown Hotel is on the extreme right of the picture which also shows the Three Greyhounds over the road on Horsefair.

The Devil's Arrows

The haunting Devil's Arrows are three standing stones or menhirs approximately 660 feet to the east of the A1(M), adjacent to Roecliffe Lane, near to where the A1 road now crosses the River Ure. They were erected in prehistoric times. The tallest stone is 22.5 foot in height, making this the tallest menhir in the United Kingdom after the 25 foot tall Rudston Monolith. It may be that the alignment originally included up to five stones. William Camden mentions four stones in his *Britannia*, noting that 'one was lately pulled downe by some that hoped, though in vaine, to finde treasure'. One was apparently displaced during a failed 'treasure hunt' during the eighteenth century and later used as the base for a nearby bridge over a river.

How did they get their name? There is a legend from 1721, that says the Devil threw the stones, aiming to hit the neighbouring town of Aldborough. He stood on Howe Hill and bellowed, 'Borobrigg keep out o' way, for Aldborough town I will ding down!' However, the stones fell short and landed near Boroughbridge instead.

The Devil's Arrows, near Boroughbridge

Market Cross and well

The fine market square has witnessed much of the history of Boroughbridge. The town's second national school was here from 1832 until 1854 when the building was sold at auction to the Conservative Association, now the town library; so were the lock-up and the stocks. The medieval St James's church was demolished in 1851, and in the next year the Battle Cross commemorating the Battle of Boroughbridge was moved from the square to Aldborough. The fountain which was built over an artesian well in 1875 (visible here) was the town's main source of water.

The well in use at Market Cross

Catton

These two delightful photos show a somewhat comfortable family posing for the photographer at the 'Old Rectory' near Stamford Bridge.

The Catton family with a rocking horse, above,
and a vintage pram, below

Copmanthorpe

The Roman road from York to Tadcaster runs to the north of the village centre, along what are now Top Lane, Hallcroft Lane and Colton Lane. The Lord of Copmanthorpe Manor was an Anglo-Saxon, named Gospatrick, at the time of the Norman invasion.

It appears in the Domesday Book as Copemantorp, from Old Norse Kaupmanna þorp, meaning Traders' Village or Craftsmen's Village. Copmanthorpe was the site of a preceptory of the Knights Templar, on land given to the Templar Knights by the Malbis family. A Preceptor, Robert de Reygate, of the Temple is recorded as early as 1291.

The railway station: off peak

Copmanthorpe street life

The Royal Oak, Main Street, Copmanthorpe. The pub is still
serving there in Main Street. The splendid photo above shows
staff and an impressive rank of carriages. Mr Rogerson is no
doubt in the crowd and the annual show advertised on the
wall still runs today as the carnival

Poppleton

The village features in the 972 Anglo-Saxon Chronicles as Popeltun and
in Domesday as Popeltune. The name comes from popel (pebble), and tun
(farm or hamlet), and describes the gravel bed on which the village is built.
Upper Poppleton is sometimes referred to as Land Poppleton, while Nether
Poppleton is Water Poppleton, denoting their locations in relation to the river
Ouse.

The water pump still can be seen today on the green, close to the
maypole. It was probably Poppleton's Red Lion that John Wesley visited in
1743. At this time the landlord was a Charles Hodgson, hence Hodgson
Lane. Wesley's diary entry for 18 February that year reads: 'We enquired at
Poppleton, a little town three miles beyond York, and hearing there was no

The water pump and maypole on the green

other town near, thought it best to call there.' The inn was also called the Four Mile Post and Poppleton House at various times.

A mayor of York was murdered here during the reign of Richard II. During the Civil War, in 1644, a tax of £126 plus a wagon and horses, was

Hens and cattle pecking and grazing on the village green

levied on the village by the Royalists. Their troops camped nearby the night preceding the Battle of Marston Moor, crossing the Ouse the next morning by a 'bridge of boats' at Poppleton.

There was a ferry here probably from 1089 when monks from St Mary's Abbey in York would have used it to visit their properties here and in Overton. The aptly named Isolde del Shippe is the first known ferrywoman, in 1379. Records from Trinity House in 1698 mention a ferry at Poppleton, a popular service which lasted until the 1960s, albeit in a different location, behind what is now Ferry Cottage on Main Street. The café boat was very popular; tea could also be had in the riverbank gardens of Priory House.

The thatched village shop and post office

Wheldrake

In 1609 the open fields of Wheldrake still existed. There were 58 leaseholders and 13 freeholders in the village living in 65 houses. Fifteen people rented their dwelling houses including a weaver and a miller. A windmill was on a field which is still called Millfield.

In 1773 the landlords applied to parliament to enclose the land of the manor. It was then that the land was made into enclosed farms with fences and ditches around them. In 1778–9, the body of the village church (seen in the distance) was demolished and rebuilt in the Georgian style, although the thirteenth-century stone tower was retained.

There were between 30 and 40 farmers in Wheldrake in the early part of the nineteenth century. Some lived on farms outside the village but many still had farmhouses with yards, barns and stables in the village Main Street. Crops that were grown were oats, peas, turnips and rape.

Wheldrake in the early nineteenth century

Images of Wheldrake: a rustic idyll

Wetherby

Around the time the sixth Duke of Devonshire was improving parts of the town (in preparation for its sale in 1824 to pay for Chatsworth House) the market place boasted market sheds, the Three Masons public house, the Town Hall and Court House and a blacksmith's forge. The market goes back to Henry III who granted a charter to the Knights Templar in 1240 thus giving Wetherby market status.

A Scheduled Ancient Monument and a Grade II listed structure, the bridge carried the Great North Road over the River Wharfe here until it was bypassed by the A1 in 1962. What was left of the Wharfedale Brewery can be seen in the centre to the left of the passing bus: in the First World War it was requisitioned to billet troops; it was then taken over by Oxleys mineral water company and in 1943 used to make Coca-Cola for the many American troops stationed in the area.

Wetherby Town Hall and Market Place

Wetherby Bridge

Tadcaster

The image shows Commercial Street with the Britannia pub, owned by John and William Dyson, on the left. A 1901 advert shows us that it was keen to attract the emerging cyclists' market, styling itself the 'Cyclists House – Dinners, Teas and Refreshments provided for Cyclists and Parties'. Dyson's brother William lived over the bridge at No 1 Bridge Street; he left money in his will to pay for the Salvation Army citadel in Chapel Street which was known as Dyson's Tabernacle. William Dyson was also owner of river barges. The pub was named after their 90-ton keel boat which shipped the first ever cargo of John Smith beer to Hull for delivery to Amsterdam where it won a gold medal in 1895. Baron Londesborough sold The Britannia in 1873 to John Smith's for £900: 'Public House ... stables, cowhouse and shed, cottage and warehouse, in occupation of Ann Dyson'.

John Smith was the son of a tanner from Meanwood in Leeds; he acquired the ramshackle Backhouse & Hartley Tadcaster brewery in 1847. When Lord Londesborough's estate was sold off in 1873 John Smith bought a large portion of land along Centre Lane and built a new brewery. John died in 1879 and did not see his £130,000 building which opened in 1883.

His brothers William and Samuel inherited the business and by 1890 they were producing 3000 barrels a week; Samuel's son Samuel Jnr then proceeded to re-equip the Old Brewery, re-open it in his own name in 1886 in competition with the established firm of John Smith's.

Getting the bus to Whitby in Commercial Street

John Smith's

The famous magnet trademark was registered in September 1908 in Brussels; it symbolises strength. The description on the certificate (# 43449) reads: 'cette marqueé represente un aimant surmonté du mot – Magnet'.

Knaresborough

Hanstock would have known that Knaresborough was famous for a number of things: Mother Shipton, Blind Jack and Knaresborough Castle – a compelling mixture of myth and history which would have drawn him to the historic market town. Knaresborough Castle has its origins in the fortified settlement or burg, which was referred to when the Angles named this place Knarresburg. Strategically placed on rocky ground towering over the Nidd some 120 feet below, the fort was developed as a castle by the Normans, traditionally under Serlo de Burgh, who had fought with William at Hastings. In 1130, Henry I authorised Serlo's nephew, Eustace Fitz-John, to develop the castle, and soon this was a base for hunting wild boar and deer.

The *Chronicle of John de Brompton*, tells us that the four knights who murdered the Archbishop Thomas Becket in Canterbury Cathedral on 29 December 1170 fled north and took refuge in Knaresborough Castle; their leader, Hugh de Morville, was Constable of the Castle. The *Chronicle* adds that the castle dogs declined to eat the scraps which the four murderers threw from the table.

Born at Ramsgill in Nidderdale in 1704, Eugene Aram moved to Knaresborough in 1734 and opened a school at the top of High Street, in White Horse Yard (now Park Square, off to the right on the photo here). A self-educated scholar and linguist, he became involved in a fraudulent scheme with a flax-dresser, Richard Houseman, and a young shoemaker, Daniel Clark. On 7 February 1744, Clark disappeared, and it was assumed he had absconded with the defrauded valuables. Soon afterwards, Aram paid off his debts and left Knaresborough.

In August 1758, a skeleton was discovered, buried on Thistle Hill. Houseman, accused of Clark's murder, denied that the bones were Clark's and eventually confessed that he was buried in St Robert's Cave, where he had seen Aram strike Clark down. Traced to King's Lynn, the schoolmaster was arrested and imprisoned in York Castle. In spite of his learned defence speech he was found guilty at York Assizes and, on 6 August 1759, condemned to be hanged in York, and later sent to the gallows at Knaresborough, just beyond

The market in Market Place is on the left

The High Street; Aram's school is off to the right

the Mother Shipton Inn. Two writers made Eugene Aram well known to Victorians – Thomas Hood, in *The Dream of Eugene Aram*, which vividly describes his guilty conscience, and Bulwer Lytton in a fanciful novel, *Eugene Aram*, which attempts to exonerate him.

The Gillygate–Bootham junction

∽ Miscellaneous ∾

So wide was Hanstock's lens that a number of the photographs he took defy categorisation. They nevertheless contribute to the picture of York life his other images give us. Here is a small sample of those miscellaneous images.

Gillygate was originally called 'Invico Sancti Egidi', then Giligate in 1373 after St Giles Church. The church was demolished in 1547; the Salvation Army citadel, opened by General Booth in 1882 but now redundant, stands on the site. Clarence Street houses and nearby Union Street car park were built on land in 1835 called the Horsefair; three horse fairs were held here every year. St John's University now dominates that corner with Lord Mayor's Walk.

Bootham: this elegant street was originally called Galman and extended from Bootham Bar to Marygate. No. 49 was home to Joseph Rowntree; called Lady Armstrong's Mansion it cost £4500 and included six acres of land; it was later taken over by Bootham School. W. H. Auden's house was opposite.

Queen Margaret's Arch is on the left. Named after Margaret Tudor, who stayed in York in 1503 on her way to marry James IV of Scotland. Adjacent to the Bar Walls opposite the King's Manor, it was built in 1497 as a short cut to and from St Mary's Abbey for use by Henry VII for 'his pleasure and passage to the Mynster'.

Fire Watch

Hanstock took a series of views from the top of York's highest gasometer on Foss Bank. Together these photographs gave a 360-degree view of the city. During WWII these viewpoints were used by Fire Watchers, positioned on top of the gasometer, to identify the location of bombs and incendiaries dropped on the city. These Watchers must have been somewhat apprehensive perched precariously on top of such a large volume of gas during a high explosive and incendiary bombing raid.

Fire Watch views, 1940, from atop the gasometer.
Above: looking north, the smoking chimney upper left marks the
position of Rowntree's Haxby Road factory. Below: looking south,
the large chimney still stands today. It is a listed building and
formerly served the corporation incinerator

Above: the view to the southwest with York Minster above the
town gas production plant in the foreground. Below: looking
northwest towards the northern part of the Plain of York. Lowther
Street cuts through the expanse of terraced housing in
The Groves, many of which were replaced with blocks of
flats in the 1950s

Salvage

Salvage and recycling is nothing new; indeed, we seem only now to have started to catch up on what was going on here in the 1930s. Here Thomas Hanstock records the City Council's earlier efforts to reduce waste, possibly in response to shortages brought about by WWII.

Collection of food salvage

Above: left, metal salvage, right, paper salvage

The Royal Sanitary Institute Congress, August 1912

Sanitary experts

The group photograph on this page is worthy of the title. Here are the assembled attendees of The Royal Sanitary Institute Congress, standing on the steps of the Yorkshire Museum, in August 1912. The gentleman in the centre, holding the dark hat and sporting a grey beard, is Dr Tempest Anderson, the prominent York philanthropist and surgeon. He is present in his role as President of the Yorkshire Philosophical Society who are hosting the congress.

Tempest Anderson (1846–1913) was an ophthalmic surgeon at York County Hospital; he was also an expert amateur photographer and volcanologist who witnessed the volcanic eruptions in the West Indies in 1902 and 1907. Born in York, he died on board ship in the Red Sea while returning from a trip to the volcanoes of Indonesia and the Philippines and is buried in Suez, Egypt. Tempest was President of the Yorkshire Philosophical Society in 1912 when he presented the Society with a 300-seat lecture theatre (the Tempest Anderson Hall) annexed to the Yorkshire Museum. His unrivalled photographic collection exceeds 3,000 images, many of which were taken during his travels.

The Yorkshire Philosophical Society was founded in 1822 by four York gentlemen: William Salmond (1769–1838), a retired colonel and amateur geologist; Anthony Thorpe (1759–1829); James Atkinson (1759–1839), a retired surgeon; and William Vernon (1789–1871), son of Archbishop Vernon of York, Vicar of Bishopthorpe. The first three met for the first minuted meeting of the Society on 7 December 1822: their aim was to collect together and house their collections of fossil bones, many of which had recently been discovered at Kirkdale Cave. Vernon attended the second meeting on 14 December at which the prospectus was drawn up 'to establish at York, a philosophical society, and to form a scientific library and a museum.' Such was the genesis of the Yorkshire Museum. The Society's name comes from the days when 'natural philosopher' was the term for a scientist.

First to the Hospitium …

... and then to Museum Gardens

The fine fourteenth-century half-timbered building in Museum Gardens was probably designed both as a guest house for visitors to the nearby St Mary's Abbey and as a warehouse for goods unloaded from the river nearby. There was an Elizabethan knot garden with central fountain between the Hospitium and the river.

The gardens were designed in the 'Gardenesque' style by landscape architect, Sir John Murray Naysmith in the 1830s in four acres formerly known as Manor Shore. They show off the buildings of the Museum and Abbey at their best while also providing space for displaying plant specimens in the Botanical Garden. As more and more exotic specimens were introduced, a conservatory was built to house tropical plants such as sugar cane, coffee, tea, ginger and cotton as well as orchids and epiphytes. A pond was created to accommodate a large rare water-lily, the *Victoria amazonica*. Although the pond and the conservatory are long gone, the ten-acre gardens are still a listed botanical garden and contain many varieties of trees, deciduous and evergreen, native and exotic. From 1835 until 1961 an entrance fee was charged. York Swimming Bath Company's pool opened in 1837; it was closed in 1922 and filled in, in 1969.

One of the least attractive parts of the city, at Foss Banks

In 1069 William the Conqueror dammed the River Foss near to its confluence with the Ouse to create a moat around the castle; this caused the river to flood upstream and form a large lake known as the King's Pool or the King's Fish Pond. King's Pool was an integral feature of the city's inner defences during the Middle Ages – the marsh was virtually impassable and explains why there is no city wall between Layerthorpe Postern and the Red Tower. Roman jetties, wharves and warehouses have been excavated on the river banks, indicating that water-borne transport and trade was important from Roman times. Foss Bridge, at the end of Walmgate, dates from 1811 and replaces a 1403 stone bridge and a wooden one before that. The fish shambles was here, as was the Saturday pig market (the tethering rings still exist) and the goose fair. There was a chicory works near Jewbury which processed the chicory which grew to the north east of the city.

Many of the mill workers lived in the Hungate area in some of the city's worst slum housing. Regular flooding eroded the river bank undermining the rear of Dennis Street, making a visit to the outdoor lavatories a highly

The perils of Hungate privies: 'it is an absolute slum'

dangerous activity. Hungate derives from Hundgate – street of the dogs – a common Viking street name. As a result of Seebohm Rowntree's ground-breaking *Poverty: A Study in Town Life* (1901), in 1908 and 1914 York's Medical Officer, Edmund Smith, produced reports condemning streets in Hungate and Walmgate as unfit for habitation.

> The back yards in Hope Street and Albert Street and in some other quarters can only be viewed with repulsion – they are so small and fetid, and so hemmed-in by surrounding houses and other buildings … There are no amenities; it is an absolute slum.

At the 1921 census York's population was 84,052 with 18,608 inhabited houses (i.e. 4.5 persons per dwelling). These properties were demolished in the 1930s, the residents being moved to the Tang Hall area of the city.

Walmgate was a place of great poverty, crime, alcohol-related violence and prostitution, like Hungate, for many years. The infant mortality rate was one in three before age one – as highlighted by Seebohm Rowntree's *Poverty* for which researchers visited 11,500 families and found that twenty-five per cent of the city population was visibly poor – in 'obvious want and squalor'. The pungent smell of hide, skins and fat from local industries added to the horror of the place. At the end of the 1880s there were 8,000 midden privies in York, many here and in Hungate. In Walmgate in 1913, the death rate was twenty-three per 1,000, almost twice York's average. Using powers under the 1930 Housing Act, York Corporation began to clear the slums: streets off Walmgate and in Hungate were demolished, and residents moved to new estates outside the city centre.

Tang Hall

In the early twentieth century York faced a serious housing problem with many residents living in insanitary slum housing, as above. In 1915 the Corporation purchased land in Tang Hall for the urgent building of houses. By 1925 over 350 houses had been built and were then occupied by tenants who had moved out of the city slums and by couples who had married following the end of World War I.

Tang Hall, Fourth Avenue shops, 1932

Carter Avenue

Hanstock photographed the area in 1932, showing the Fourth Avenue Shops and Carter Avenue, named after the City Alderman who was a prime mover in the 1915 land purchase.

His photographs also show that building continued after 1925; the image of Dodsworth Avenue was taken just before the properties were occupied.

Dodsworth Avenue

Archbisop Holgate's Grammar School, Lord Mayor's Walk

Lord Mayor's Walk

Lord Mayor's Walk runs beside the north-eastern city walls less than 100 yards from Hanstock's Studio in Clarence Street. In his time the two principal establishments on the Walk were Archbishop Holgate's Grammar School and the Diocesan Training College.

The Practising School and the Model School of the York and Ripon Diocesan Training College were opened in 1851 and 1859 respectively in Lord Mayor's Walk. The two schools were complementary, the best teaching methods being illustrated in the Model School for the students who then put them into practice in the other. A new combined school building was built in 1899. The college, now the University of St John, York, expanded into the Archbishop Holgate Grammar School's buildings, following the school's move to new premises on Hull Road in 1963.

The railings lining the Walk were removed during World War II to make armaments. In truth 80 per cent of railings were unsuitable for the job but this information was never revealed so as to allow those who 'donated' them to believe they were helping the war effort. Much of the iron now rests on the bed of the North Sea (ironically called the German Ocean until the early twentieth century).

The Model School, Lord Mayor's Walk

Lord Mayor's Walk, south east

Lord Mayor's Walk, north west

A serious case of overloading while Mr Leeman looks away

The Little John, Castlegate. The Little John is on the left with its graphic sign; the Castle Hotel is over the road on the corner of Friargate, with its Music Lounge. It opened in 1851, formerly as the Wheatsheaf, and closed in 1969

Before reverting to the Blue Boar, this pub was called the Little John; the original Blue Boar closed in 1775 but some historians argue that the Little John and the Blue Boar were entirely different and that the Little John was previously known as the Robin Hood from the 1700s, changing its name to Little John in 1893. At that time, a sign was placed in the pub, reading: 'Robin Hood is dead and gone, now come and drink with Little John.'

The oldest continuously licensed premises in York are:

1. Olde Starre, Stonegate – 1644

2. Golden Fleece, Pavement – 1668

3. Old White Swan, Goodramgate – 1703

4. Robin Hood (formerly Little John), Castlegate – 1733

5. Punch Bowl, Stonegate – 1761

6. Windmill, Blossom Street – 1770

The marriage of Helen Faith Grey and Captain Gardner
at the Minster in 1910

৯৯ People ৯৯

PEOPLE MAKE A PLACE, EVEN WHEN they are anonymous. Here are some of York's people, the details of whom are largely obscure. So who were they? We learn from the press cutting shown below that Mrs Gardener died in 1949, and that her husband attained the rank of Lt. Colonel, was awarded the CBE and died in 1962; they lived in Grays Court, hence the Minster wedding as they were in the Minster parish, so to speak.

Grays Court is probably the oldest continuously occupied house in the country; parts of it date back to 1080 when it was commissioned by the first Norman Archbishop of York, Thomas de Bayeux. Grays Court was the original Treasurer's House. It exudes history: James I dined here with Edmund, Lord Sheffield, the Lord President of the North, knighting eight noblemen in the Long Gallery in one evening. Sir Thomas Fairfax owned Grays Court between 1649 and 1663, during which time he laid siege to the city. James Duke of York and Maria Beatrix of Modena, his wife, later King and Queen, stayed in Grays Court in 1679.

Elizabeth Robinson was born here in 1718. She founded the Blue-stocking Club 'where literary topics were to be discussed, but politics, gossip and card-playing were barred'. How wise.

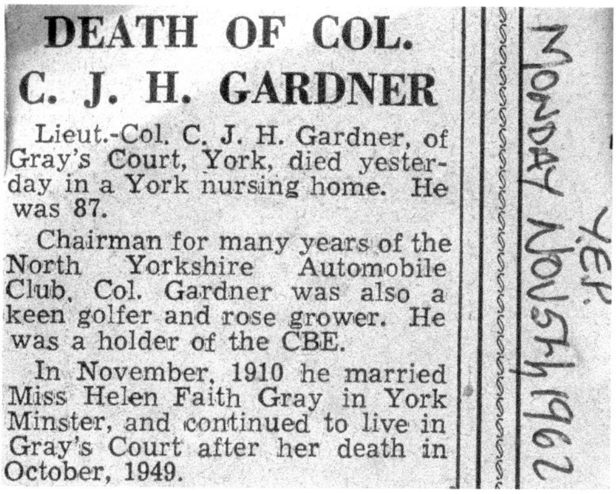

Press cutting reporting the death of Lt Colonel Gardner

DEATH OF COL. C. J. H. GARDNER

Lieut.-Col. C. J. H. Gardner, of Gray's Court, York, died yesterday in a York nursing home. He was 87.

Chairman for many years of the North Yorkshire Automobile Club, Col. Gardner was also a keen golfer and rose grower. He was a holder of the CBE.

In November, 1910 he married Miss Helen Faith Gray in York Minster, and continued to live in Gray's Court after her death in October, 1949.

MONDAY NOV 5TH 1962

The images on the following pages show six delightful special occasion groups, the details of which are unknown and will probably remain so. The girl on the far right in the image at the bottom of this page is wearing a Rowntree's costume

The Monkgate Methodist Chapel congregation

Motor cars outside the Minster

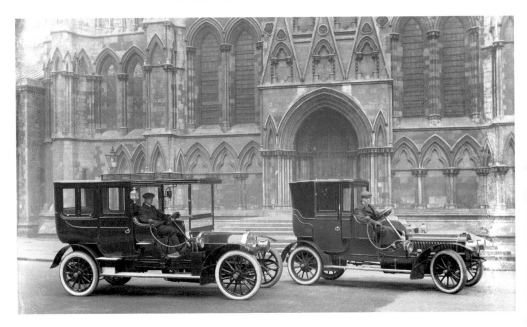

The Monkgate Methodist Chapel

In 1864 the Primitive Methodist Conference was held in York, by now one of the principal circuit towns. Ebenezer Chapel was the most important Primitive Methodist chapel in York. The chapel lasted for fifty years until it closed in 1901 when York inhabitants started to move out to the suburbs. In 1903 the Monkgate Primitive Methodist Church was officially opened, replacing the Ebenezer Chapel. From 1901, when Ebenezer Chapel was sold, until 1903, when Monkgate Chapel was opened, the congregation used the Victoria Hall, Goodramgate, for its services.

The motor car and tram service

The motor car was to be a constant and annoying presence until 1991. In 1901 York Minster gave permission for Deangate to pass close to the South Transept, linking Goodramgate with Duncombe Place and High Petergate. In time this led to over 2,000 noisy and polluting vehicles per hour passing close to the Minster. Deangate was finally closed to traffic in 1991.

Laying the tram lines opposite the station

The laying of electric tram lines in 1910 signalled the replacement of the horse-drawn trams. In 1900 there had been eleven such trams drawn by horses from a pool of thirty-three. The tram lines were all taken up again in 1935 as car use increased. The last journey from Nessgate on 16 November was witnessed by large crowds gathered at midnight to watch the Lord Mayor and Inspector J. Stewart – the driver of the very first service – drive York trams into oblivion. The electrification cost £89,741; over eight miles of track were laid.

The first day of the tram service, 20 January 1910, saw 6,786 passengers carried with fares totalling £35 18s. 5d. – as the fare was 2d., fare dodging must have been rife. Rail cars (as trams were called) plied between Fulford and South Bank; Fulford and Acomb; Haxby Road and South Bank and Haxby Road and Acomb – and vice versa on a ten-minute service between 8.00 am and 10.45, plus works specials; 2s. 10d. on Sundays. The universal fare was 2d. (less than 1p) per journey.

Early York firefighters

York Minster bell ringers

The York Minster Society of Change Ringers are the people who ring those bells on Sundays and practise on Tuesday evenings, creating a marvellous sound which produces a fitting soundtrack to the city of York. The carillon is rung every day to announce Evensong. The two western towers of York Minster contain between them a total of 56 bells, the largest number of bells in any English cathedral.

The 10.8-ton Great Peter arrived back at York Minster in 1914 after restoration; ten horses were required to pull the cart. The bell was originally cast by John Taylor & Co of Loughborough in 1840 and is Britain's second biggest bell after Great Paul – which Taylor's also cast (9 feet high and weighing seventeen tons) and hangs in St Paul's Cathedral. Great Peter is the heaviest of the Minster's ring of twelve bells but, despite its weight, can be swung and rung by one person. It is the deepest-toned bell in Europe. Taylor's was established in 1784 and still trades today. The bells were restored and returned here in March 1914 by John Warner & Sons Ltd from their Spitalfields Bell Foundry.

Minster bell ringers: some earnest-looking campanologists here.
The contraption on the table is a telephone

The Sword and Mace bearers outside York's medieval Guildhall. In the fourteenth century King Richard III granted a Royal Charter and other privileges to the City of York. The mayor of the city was henceforth to be proceeded by a Swordbearer and a Macebearer, when he was out and about in the city. This privilege is now only exercised on ceremonial occasions. The present sword dates from 1437 and has been subject to a number of later embellishments. The present mace was made in 1647

York Railway Station

At the outbreak of WWI all the main line railways fell under the control of the Railway Executive Committee, thus effectively nationalising them. British railways performed a feat of biblical proportions just in the week from 10 to 17 August 1914: 68,847 men, 21,523 horses, 166 guns, 2,446 vehicles, 1,368 bicycles and 2,550 tonnes of baggage and stores were shipped from the UK to France by rail. 184,475 railway workers joined up while many thousands more stayed in the UK to build the vehicles and to keep the railways running. About a third of railway staff were called up and freight tonnage doubled; passenger traffic was increased due to the movements of service personnel and rolling stock was requisitioned.

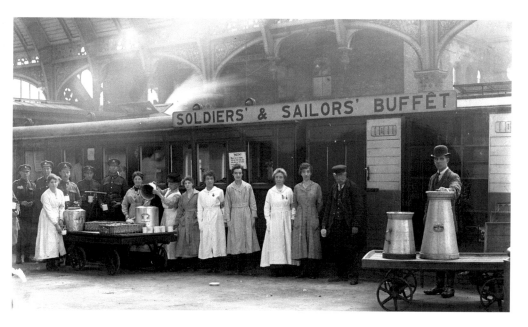

A canteen for travelling troops on York Railway Station

A lady and maid

Serious overcrowding on a boat: conference delegates
on their way to Bishopthorpe Palace

The bowls club in Clarence Gardens

We end where we came in, with a snowy scene of York

Endword

Beware how you destroy your antiquities, guard them with religious care! They are what give you a decided character and superiority over other provincial cities. You have lost much, take care of what remains.

William Etty 1787–1849

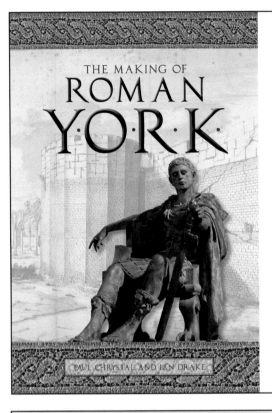